Stop Worrying

Understand Your Anxiety— and Banish It Forever!

Frank J. Bruno, Ph.D.

Macmillan • USA

Life's Little Keys

Self-Help Strategies for a Happier, Healthier You

ADDITIONAL TITLES

Conquer Shyness

Stop Procrastinating

Defeat Depression

Conquer Loneliness

Get a Good Night's Sleep

*To those who struggle
with the problem of excessive worry*

Macmillan General Reference
A Simon & Schuster Macmillan Company
1633 Broadway
New York, NY 10019-6785

An Arco Book

MACMILLAN is a registered trademark of Macmillan, Inc.
ARCO is a registered trademark of Prentice-Hall, Inc.

ISBN: 0-02-861301-5
Library of Congress Card Catalog Number 96-085323

Manufactured in the United States of America

10 9 8 7 6 5 4 3 2 1

Cover design by Kevin Hanek
Book design by Scott Meola

CONTENTS

Preface   vii

Acknowledgments   viii

1   *The Anatomy of Anxiety:* Looking at Chronic Worry   I

2   *Exploring Bodily Processes:* Do You Have Weak Nerves or Low Blood Sugar?   13

3   *Our Emotional Conflicts:* Understanding the Inner Struggle   27

4   *The Worry Habit:* What Has Been Learned Can Be Unlearned   45

5   *Inducing Relaxation:* Low Arousal Can't Coexist With Worry   65

6   *Our Mental Lives:* "I Think, Therefore I Worry"   79

7   *Everybody Worries:* Looking at the Human Plight We're All In   95

8   *Psychotherapy:* The Talking Cure   III

9   *Tranquilizers:* The Pros and Cons of Antianxiety Drugs   121

10   *Life Can Be Better:* A Seven-Step Antiworry Program   129

PREFACE

There is no advice in this world more glib than, "Don't worry about it."

When we are given this advice, we either answer or think, "I would like to stop worrying if I could. But that's just the problem—I *can't!*"

Worrying, unlike walking across a room, does not seem to be under the direct control of the will. It appears to be involuntary, beyond the power of choice. Consequently, we often feel that we are worry's victims.

Stop Worrying shows you that you don't have to be the emotional pawn of your own anxieties. It demonstrates precisely how it is possible to bring excessive, chronic worry under voluntary control.

The book accomplishes its purpose by offering you (1) insight into the process of worry and (2) practical, self-directed coping strategies designed to reduce your level of anxiety.

If chronic worry is a problem in your life, take heart. This book offers you realistic hope, hope based on both my own life experiences and sound psychological information.

ACKNOWLEDGMENTS

A number of people have helped me make *Stop Worrying* a reality. My thanks are expressed to:

Barbara Gilson, senior editor at Macmillan, for her recognition of the value of the book and for being a supportive and creative editor.

Jennifer Perillo, editor at Macmillan, for her assistance and for her appreciation of the book's themes.

George J. McKeon, artist, for his capturing of key ideas in cartoon form.

Bert Holtje, my agent, for encouraging the development of the book.

My wife, Jeanne, for our many meaningful discussions.

My son, Franklin, for our conversations about language and meaning.

George K. Zaharoupoulos, a true teaching colleague, for his steadfast encouragement of my writing projects.

1 THE ANATOMY OF ANXIETY: LOOKING AT CHRONIC WORRY

Thousands of moviegoers were amused by the obsessive-compulsive antics of Bill Murray playing the part of the title character in *What About Bob?* Bob Wiley was plagued by irrational fears—phobias—that he could only fight off to some extent by rigidly following various magical rituals. The film shows him cleverly turning the tables on his psychiatrist, making a pompous person into Bob's victim.

However, a moment's reflection suggests that the only real victim of an actual obsessive-compulsive disorder is the person who has it.

Why are we entertained by films like *What About Bob?* We find Murray's portrayal amusing because the story presents us with a magnification mirror, one that takes a close-up look at our own flaws, and then blows them up into a caricature of themselves. We laugh because we are looking at a cartoon version of ourselves.

I worry.

You worry.

We all worry.

To worry is to be human. Then why am I writing, and why should you be interested in reading, a book called *Stop Worrying*? If it is human to worry, maybe we should stop here, bow our heads to the harsh blows of fear and anxiety, and just accept our human fate.

This might be an acceptable approach if the level of anxiety, the amount of worry, was always realistic and appropriate to our actual circumstances. But often it is not. Everyone recognizes that Bob exaggerates his fears.

To some extent, perhaps most of us are prone to do the same.

In other words, we want to eliminate *excessive* worry, *irrational* worry, and *chronic* worry. Of course, we can't eliminate *all* worry. This in fact should *not* be your goal. But you *do* want to eliminate the kind of worry that makes you suffer for no reason, that poisons your life, that ages you prematurely.

This book will help you to:

1. Understand worry.

2. Eliminate its adverse impact on your life.

Varieties of Worry

Daniel G. is driving down the highway toward a favorite resort area. His wife and two young daughters are with him in the car. The day is sunny, and the family is in a cheerful mood. Suddenly, for no apparent reason, Daniel has the thought, "What if we have a blowout on one of the front tires? My God, we could flip over end to end." A mental movie is projected on the screen of his mind. He sees his wife and children trapped in the car and burning to death. He glances over at his wife. She is relaxed and trusting, as if they are completely safe and nothing can happen.

Daniel's heart begins to pound, his palms are damp, and he wants to pull over to the side of the road. He is in the grips of an all-consuming dread. Only brute will-power enables him to keep driving and not give in to his irrational fear.

What is happening? What is Daniel going through? How can we explain his emotional state? And, how can Daniel cope in the most effective manner? This book will provide answers to these questions, and more. For the present, in this chapter it will be useful to explore the varieties of worry, or more correctly, kinds of anxiety reactions.

≋≋ ≋≋ ≋≋ ≋≋ ≋≋ ≋≋ ≋≋ ≋≋

REALISTIC ANXIETY

Realistic anxiety is anxiety that is appropriate to a situation. Let's say that you find yourself in an unfamiliar area of a large city. The region is run down, some of the people look angry and unkempt, and you have lost your way. If your heart begins to race, or you are tempted to break into a run, this is certainly understandable. You are experiencing the well known *fight-or-flight* reaction identified about eighty years ago by the physiologist Walter B. Cannon. The reaction prepares the body for action, puts it on what Cannon sometimes called a "war footing."

Adrenal hormones are pumped into the bloodstream. Digestion slows down so that more blood can be sent to the muscles in the arms and the legs. You are in a state of alarm. You are vigilant and on guard.

Now let's say that someone actually stops you, holds a gun to your head, and demands money. If your heart beats faster still, it is understandable.

What you are experiencing is simply *fear*. The word *fear* and the term *realistic anxiety* are completely interchangeable.

There are many situations in life that evoke a fear response. No one in his or her right mind thinks that we should eliminate all fear.

Realistic anxiety is like a red light flashing on your dashboard. It is a warning signal.

Note that, in general, realistic anxiety tends to be present oriented. It tells us that there is an actual threat *here and now*. As we will see, this is not true of neurotic anxiety, the kind of anxiety that underlies chronic worry.

EXISTENTIAL ANXIETY

Before we proceed to a discussion of neurotic anxiety, let's take a look at existential anxiety, a first cousin to realistic anxiety. Realistic anxiety and existential anxiety are related because they are both part and parcel of the human condition. Neurotic anxiety, as we shall see, is different. It is a kind of psychological graft on life, and an unnecessary one.

Existential anxiety is just what it sounds like, anxiety about existence itself. In other words, it is uneasiness about the human predicament. What is meant by the two words *human predicament*? Just this: We know that we can, and in fact someday *will*, die. We also know that we are prone to aging, disease, and injury from accidents. Existential anxiety is intrinsic to life. It is normal from time to time to have a sense of dread about the future.

Existential philosophers, thinkers who write and speculate on the nature of human experience, have had a lot to say about the unhappiness associated with existential anxiety. And they have offered practical suggestions for reducing and resisting its corrosive effects on our lives. There will be more about this in Chapter 7.

These words excerpted from Barbara Q's journal, a patient in psychotherapy, suggest what the experience of existential anxiety is like:

Here I am, a relatively young person in good health, the mother of three lovely children. I like my role as a mother. I like my job as a grammar school teacher. I love my husband. The sun is shining, the grass is green. All seems right with the world.

And yet. . .

And yet. . .

And yet I realize how transient it all is. It all seems like some sort of illusion. A hundred years from now we'll all be corpses rotting in our graves. Maybe I'll die young of some terrible illness like my best friend, Mabel. Maybe I'll suffer and suffer. Why does it have to be like this?

Why do we have to suffer? What's it all about? Who or what designed this absurd comedy we call life?

We will return to Barbara's journal in a future chapter. Let us simply note at this point that she is expressing a high level of existential anxiety.

Although existential anxiety *is* normal, it can reach abnormal levels of intensity. This is because existential anxiety unfortunately interacts with neurotic anxiety. When existential anxiety and neurotic anxiety join, they have a multiplicative effect on each other, and the general level of personal anxiety blossoms to an unacceptable degree.

NEUROTIC ANXIETY

Neurotic anxiety is anxiety that is unrealistic, irrational, and completely useless. It is useless because it does not help you solve a problem or cope effectively with a situation. It just drags you down, down, down into deep psychological waters until you feel that you are emotionally drowning.

Sigmund Freud, the father of psychoanalysis, made an intense study of neurotic anxiety. Freud believed that virtually all neurotic anxiety has its roots in a conflict between (1) forbidden desires of either a sexual or aggressive nature and (2) the moral code of family and culture. Although there is much of value in Freud's approach, it is important to realize that Freud died in 1939. Much has been learned in the more than fifty years since his death. Consequently, there is more than one way to explain neurotic anxiety. Future chapters expand on this point.

Let's identify the principal kinds of anxiety disorders, disorders in which a neurotic process plays a paramount role. These maladies are set forth in *The Diagnostic and Statistical Manual of Mental Disorders* published by the American Psychiatric Association. Although the word *disorder* is used, you should realize that these conditions range from mild to severe, from acute to chronic. In many cases, if you suffer from excessive anxiety, there is much you can do for yourself. So don't let the word *disorder* frighten you too much. It's just a label, and maybe a questionable one.

An *obsessive-compulsive disorder* is characterized by an obsessive idea that causes anxiety; this is followed in time by a magical ritual designed to reduce the level of anxiety. The obsessive idea and the magical ritual are both regarded as irrational to some degree by the troubled person. The fictional Bob Wiley, described in the opening paragraph of this chapter, suffered from an obsessive-compulsive disorder.

Inventor Nikola Tesla, the man who made alternating current practical, was unable to conceal an obsessive-compulsive disorder from curious observers. Tesla, a lifelong bachelor, used to eat almost every night for a number of years in the same dining room of a certain elegant hotel. He had to have at his disposal exactly eight white linen napkins so he could wipe away the germs from his drinking glasses, plates, and silverware. He knew that his action pattern was unable to eliminate microbes effectively, but nonetheless he had to engage in his behavioral ritual or he could not eat in comfort.

A *phobic disorder*, or *phobia*, has as its key feature an irrational fear. There are three basic kinds of phobic disorders: (1) agoraphobia, (2) specific phobia, and (3) social phobia. *Agoraphobia* is characterized by an intense desire to stay in control of circumstances. The individual works at staying out of situations where it would be difficult or impossible to make a voluntary departure. Consequently the individual tends to want to stay close to home and avoid crowded places. The individual also has a dislike of public transportation (for example, riding on a bus) because, again, the lack of actual control over the vehicle induces feelings of helplessness.

Specific phobia has as its distinctive feature an irrational fear of a specific thing or circumstance such as a fear of snakes or cats or the night.

The outstanding attribute of *social phobia* is extreme anxiety associated with the reactions and judgments of other people. The individual suffering from this phobia is particularly concerned about being humiliated in social situations. Common shyness and social phobia are, of course, very similar. However, a person is not considered to be suffering from a social phobia in the clinical sense unless he or she experiences significant impairment of the quality of daily life as well as an extreme and persistent anxiety.

A *panic disorder* suggests that the individual "goes to pieces" in certain situations. In extreme cases the person begins to hyperventilate or becomes faint. A somewhat less severe case is provided by Marie R., an adult returning to college after a seven-year break. When she takes an algebra exam she says that her "mind goes blank." She cannot solve problems that she could have solved easily when studying at home.

A *post-traumatic stress disorder* is characterized by anxiety associated with memories of past events, events that were emotionally traumatic. If you survived a terrifying flood, earthquake, fire, tornado, or accident, it is understandable that from time to time you might involuntarily reflect on your frightening experience and reactivate the original fright. Under these conditions we may speak of *flashbacks*. A post-traumatic stress disorder may also induce nightmares, digestive disturbances, and other symptoms.

A *generalized anxiety disorder* is one in which the anxiety seems to arise without much rhyme or reason. There is no clear single source of one's dread. The term used to describe this unpleasant state of emotional affairs is *free-floating anxiety*. It is as if an almost visible gray cloud of apprehension floats over the person's head and follows him or her everywhere.

The clinical term *generalized anxiety disorder* is more or less synonymous with the everyday word *worrywart*. *The American Heritage Dictionary of the English Language*, Third Edition, defines a worrywart as "one who worries excessively and needlessly." A worrywart is a person who can worry—and worry and worry and worry—just about any old time about any old thing. Daniel G., the man who began to worry about a blowout while driving to a resort area, is a worrywart. He worries, more or less at random, about his health, paying bills, offending people, earthquakes, inflation, his job, how to enjoy himself when he has some time off, and so forth.

This book is designed to help you cope with anxiety disorders in their various guises.

My Own Story

If you are a worrywart, if you can relate to some degree to the variety of anxiety disorders already identified, I sympathize with you. I have been a worrywart, too, and I have suffered from difficult-to-deal-with anxiety. I know what it is to worry about almost anything.

This is one of the reasons I was attracted to psychology as a field of study and as a vocation. An important aim was to help myself. I have more than once told close friends, "Well, there's one person who was definitely helped by my study of psychology and psychotherapy, and that's me." I have been to some extent my own best client. Those of you who read one of my earlier books, *Think Yourself Thin*, know that I once weighed 245 pounds (when I was twenty years old). I ate partly to reduce anxiety. One of food's effects is that it is a natural tranquilizer. It activates the parasympathetic division of the autonomic nervous system in such a way that arousal is lowered. This action is antagonistic to anxiety, and can become a habitual self-defeating way of dealing with it.

I took my first class in abnormal psychology at the University of California at Los Angeles (UCLA). My professor was James C. Coleman, author of a well-known textbook, *Abnormal Psychology and Modern Life*. Some of the insights I gained from this course played a crucial role in learning to come to grips with my own excessive worry.

Am I worry-free now? Do I take "no thought for the morrow?" Do I live in a bland "here and now" with no vigilance and respect for the dangers of the future? Of course not. However, I am no longer a chronic worrier. My anxiety is within tolerable bounds. I have learned to cope. And when I forget to use some of the strategies that I will share with you in this book, and my anxiety begins to rise, I quickly put myself into an action designed to restore my emotional balance.

If you like, you can call me a *recovering worrywart*. The process goes on. And I, like you, am a companion on the road of learning.

How This Book Can Help You

Stop Worrying can help you in your process of recovery from chronic worry by offering a set of explicit self-directed coping strategies. The strategies are presented in the form of practical tips, tips that you can readily and easily apply to yourself in daily living.

The coping strategies are directed to various levels and aspects of the tendency toward excessive worry. As you read through the book it will become evident to you which coping strategies will be applicable and useful in your own life.

It is easy to give advice. It is more difficult to give *sound* advice. And when sound advice *is* given, it is important to follow up the advice with sensible reasons in support of it. None of these points is ignored in the material to follow. You will see very clearly why certain strategies are offered and why they are likely to work.

You don't have to be a perfect person for the suggestions in this book to work for you. There are no perfect people. You don't have be free of all of your hang-ups to reduce your level of useless worry. No one is free of all of his or her hang-ups.

You only have to possess (1) a mind open to learning and (2) a willingness to apply the self-directed coping strategies to your daily life. Given these two factors, you will find that this book offers you real hope.

Start hoping.

Start coping.

Take your first steps toward freeing yourself from the burden of excessive worry.

Key Points to Remember

▫— This book will help you to (1) understand worry and (2) eliminate its adverse impact on your life.

▫— *Realistic anxiety* is anxiety that is appropriate to a situation.

▫— The *fight-or-flight* reaction prepares the body for action.

▫—␣ The word *fear* and the term *realistic anxiety* are completely interchangeable.

▫—␣ *Existential anxiety* is anxiety about existence itself.

▫—␣ *Neurotic anxiety* is anxiety that is unrealistic, irrational, and completely useless.

▫—␣ An *obsessive-compulsive disorder* is characterized by an obsessive idea that causes anxiety followed in time by a magical ritual designed to reduce the level of anxiety.

▫—␣ A *phobic disorder*, or *phobia*, has as its key feature an irrational fear.

▫—␣ A *post-traumatic stress disorder* is characterized by anxiety associated with memories of past events, events that were emotionally traumatic.

▫—␣ A *generalized anxiety disorder* is one in which the anxiety seems to arise without much rhyme or reason. *Free-floating anxiety* is present when there is no clear single source of one's dread.

▫—␣ The clinical term *generalized anxiety disorder* is more or less synonymous with the everyday word *worrywart*.

▫—␣ *Stop Worrying* offers you a set of explicit self-directed coping strategies that will help you in your process of recovery from chronic worry.

2 EXPLORING BODILY PROCESSES: DO YOU HAVE WEAK NERVES OR LOW BLOOD SUGAR?

Imagine a piano standing alone on the stage of a large, empty concert hall.

A pianist enters, sits down at the bench, and begins to play what is intended to be a beautiful song. The song fills the air of the hall. However, it is *not* beautiful. It is full of irritating discord. Why? The piano is in poor condition. The hammers do not strike properly. The felts are deteriorated. The strings are loose. The whole instrument is out of tune.

Your brain and nervous system are like the piano. In fact your whole biological being is like the piano. If your organic functioning is below normal, you will be neither able to think clearly nor enjoy a stable emotional life.

The piano-melody analogy is one way to "solve" the classical mind-body problem in philosophy. The body, including the brain and nervous system, is the organ—the instrument—of mind. Although the mind is intangible and insubstantial like the melody, it exists as a result of the *activity* of the organ. You can't produce a beautiful song with an out-of-condition piano. And you can't have an optimal mental and emotional life with a poorly functioning organism.

Vanessa says, "I don't know what's wrong with me. I worry about every little thing. I'm a nervous wreck. And I can't seem to do anything about it."

Her friend Judith answers, "Gee. Maybe you're neurotic. Maybe you should see a psychologist or something."

With a gloomy look at her companion, Vanessa says, "Yeah. Maybe you're right." Then she finishes the doughnut and soft drink she is having for breakfast at Big Daddy's Big Doughnut Factory.

Yes, maybe Vanessa *is* neurotic. And yes, maybe she should see a psychologist if her worry is chronic. On the other hand, I'm a psychologist, and I'm wondering about that doughnut and soft drink Vanessa's having for breakfast. Could Vanessa's dietary habits be a cause of her mental state? If not the principal cause, could it be an aggravating cause? Perhaps Vanessa is inducing a state of hypoglycemia. But I'm getting ahead of my story, and I'll have more to say about hypoglycemia later.

The approach taken in this chapter is actually very traditional. It is based on the assumption that biological processes underlie psychological events. More than two thousand years ago Hippocrates, often called the father of medicine, said that four humors (fluids) caused our basic personality traits. If your humors were out of balance you were in a "bad humor." If your humors were in balance, you were in a "good humor." And the language persists until this day. Although Hippocrates had the details wrong, his approach is first cousin to the modern idea that biochemistry has something to do with your moods.

The terms *psychosomatic* and *behavioral medicine* are also sometimes used to describe this chapter's viewpoint.

About a hundred years ago neurotic people were thought to have "weak nerves." The condition was called *neurasthenia*, which means nothing more than—what else?—"weak nerves." However, the vast majority of people who worry, suffer from irrational anxiety, and live with excessive nervous tension, don't have anything really wrong with their nerves. When someone says, "I must have weak nerves," this has no scientific meaning. It must be taken as a metaphor. The individual is really saying, "It's *as if* I have weak nerves." In other words, the actual

nervous system is potentially strong, but it is functioning in a questionable manner.

Although the approach taken in the book as a whole is psychological, not biological, it will pay us to explore possible ways to correct or enhance your biological, or organic, functioning. This will make it much easier for your to improve your mental and emotional state.

As the opening paragraphs of this chapter suggest, the mind and the body *interact*. They affect each other in complex ways, and this insight should not be ignored.

What You Can Do For Yourself

The balance of the chapter will present practical things you can do to enhance the kind of bodily processes that will undercut worry.

HYPOGLYCEMIA

The term *hypoglycemia* means "low blood sugar." When glucose levels fall below an optimal level, then one is in a state of hypoglycemia. When in this state it is quite possible that one may experience "weak nerves." A migraine headache, a feeling of having no energy, an inability to concentrate, and, of course, anxiety are some of the symptoms associated with hypoglycemia.

If blood sugar falls too low, one can lapse into a coma. And the condition can even be life-threatening. But I'm not talking about excessively pathological hypoglycemia. Perhaps the condition I'm describing can best be summarized with the words *subclinical hypoglycemia*. In fact it's a controversial condition, and there isn't much consensus among physicians, psychiatrists, psychologists, and the mental health community in general regarding its importance. I'm being honest with you in telling you this. So let's not overemphasize its importance.

Nonetheless, having said this, it is a reasonable *working hypothesis* to suggest that chronic low blood sugar of the subclinical variety may be a contributing factor in some cases of chronic worry. It might be in your case. So the hypothesis merits consideration.

The nice thing about the recommendations for self-treatment of hypoglycemia is that they all involve healthful dietary changes. Hippocrates's advice in the treatment of medical conditions was, "First, do no harm." Well, even if you *don't* have hypoglycemia or a tendency toward it, it will do no harm to make the kinds of changes associated with its treatment.

Avoid or Restrict Dietary Sugar. Dietary sugar in the form of sucrose is a contributing cause to hypoglycemia. This may seem odd in view of the fact that the problem is *low* blood sugar. Wouldn't it seem that taking in *extra* sugar would help the problem? But it doesn't work that way. Excessive sugar in food tends to have the effect of quickly raising the blood sugar. This quick rise sets up a kind of panic reaction in the hypothalamus (a center that regulates biological drives in the brain). A message is sent down the spinal cord to the pancreas that says, "Secrete insulin." Because it is a panic situation, the pancreas often *oversecretes* insulin, and the blood sugar plummets.

The whole process described above is called *the hypoglycemic rebound*. It reminds one of a ball hitting a backstop. The harder you throw the ball, the harder it bounces back. Similarly, the more sugar you take in at a time, the bigger the reactive drop in blood sugar.

Perhaps you protest, "I don't eat that much sugar. I only use a teaspoon in my coffee. And I seldom have more than three cups of coffee a day."

All right. However, there is a concept known as *hidden sugar*. This is the sugar that lurks in doughnuts, cakes, cookies, pies, candy bars, soft drinks, ice cream, jams, jellies, syrup, and so forth. It has been estimated that looked at in this way, the average American adult eats anywhere from fifty to one hundred pounds of sugar a year!

In fact, adult onset diabetes, a condition known as Type II diabetes, is on the rise in the United States. And it is quite likely that the American style of eating, a diet high in sugar and refined carbohydrates, contributes to it.

Restrict Refined Carbohydrates. Refined carbohydrates consist of foods that are high in carbohydrates and low in fiber. Examples include white flour, white rice, mashed potatoes, and french fries. Note that white flour is included in many breads, cakes, pie crusts, pancakes, and .

waffles. White flour is not sugar. But it is quickly digested by the body and metabolized into sugar. This becomes glucose in the blood stream and is a contributing factor to the hypoglycemic rebound.

Use Coffee and Drinks Containing Caffeine in Moderation. Caffeine is a stimulant. It acts upon the pancreas in such a way as to induce it to secrete insulin. The excessive secretion of insulin contributes to the hypoglycemic rebound.

If you think you are somewhat prone to hypoglycemia, don't drink coffee with high sugar or high refined carbohydrate foods. This is why I gave the example of Vanessa, who ate a doughnut and a soft drink for breakfast. In terms of the effect on her blood sugar such a meal is a disaster. (Note that many soft drinks contain a high level of caffeine.)

It is not a good idea to drink coffee or a caffeine-laden soft drink on an empty stomach. This too induces negative alterations in your blood sugar. It is best to take these beverages with slowly digested food.

Increase Your Intake of Complex Carbohydrates and Proteins. These are the foods that, as indicated above, are slowly digested. It takes the body longer to extract sugar from complex carbohydrates and proteins than from refined carbohydrates. And this time lapse allows for blood sugar to stabilize itself at optimal levels.

Foods high in complex carbohydrates include whole grain breads, whole grain cereals, whole grain rice, vegetables, legumes, and fresh fruits. (When fruit is converted to jam or jelly, or canned in sugar and water, it edges over toward the refined carbohydrate category.)

Foods high in protein include milk, cheese, dairy products in general, eggs, beef, chicken, fish. Beans, included in the legume family, are a rich source of both complex carbohydrates and protein. Beef, chicken, and fish are sources primarily of protein, not complex carbohydrates.

Peanut butter presents an interesting individual case. A peanut is not a nut, but a legume. Consequently, peanut butter is a high-protein food with complex carbohydrate

value. A teaspoon of peanut butter on a half slice of whole wheat toast makes a snack that helps to stabilize blood sugar.

As you can see, even if you are not prone to hypoglycemia, the kinds of dietary changes associated with its treatment tend to be generally helpful. Consequently, it is safe to give these changes a try to see if they produce positive alterations in your emotional life.

STIMULANTS

Use Stimulants in Moderation. Stimulants are chemical agents that tend to increase central nervous system arousal. They make you more alert and active. Interestingly, the drugs that are prescribed to reduce anxiety are designed to induce a state of muscle relaxation and lowered arousal. They have a sedating effect and are the opposite of stimulants. Consequently, based on the old principle that "an ounce of prevention is worth

a pound of cure," it makes sense to avoid or restrict stimulants.

Again, caffeine is a stimulant. I am writing about it here, however, in terms of a different function from what I was writing about it earlier. The earlier comments related to blood sugar. Now the point is being made that caffeine, independent of its effect on blood sugar, is a stimulant. It is usually said that caffeine is a "cerebral stimulant," meaning it makes your brain more alert and may even help you to think more clearly. I am not telling you to stop using caffeine. I'm only recommending that it be used in moderation. At this moment, as I'm writing this, I have a cup of coffee on my desk.

Perhaps it would be a good idea to define *moderation*. Two or three cups of coffee a day, spaced out with food, is moderate usage. Ten or twelve cups of coffee a day, often consumed on an empty stomach, is immoderate usage. It is well known that too much coffee can cause what has been nicknamed "coffee nerves."

Nicotine is a stimulant found in cigarettes, cigars, and chewing tobacco. Note that chewing tobacco, although it is spit out, still allows for the entry of substantial amounts of nicotine into the bloodstream via tissue absorption in the mouth. General health problems aside, nicotine should be used in moderation if you are prone to be a worrier. Chain smoking can induce a state of nicotine toxicity that can really aggravate any tendency toward anxiety.

Amphetamines ("speed," "pep pills," and "uppers") should be avoided completely for recreational purposes. Although amphetamines have legitimate uses in the treatment of certain conditions such as attention deficit disorder in children and some adults, compulsive eating, and a tendency to fall asleep at inappropriate times, amphetamines should not be taken for "kicks" or to obtain a cheap thrill. Considering anxiety, they tend to aggravate it. In cases of persons who really abuse amphetamines, behavioral symptoms include great emotional agitation and motor restlessness.

The same general statements made about avoiding amphetamines be made about cocaine. Cocaine, like amphetamines, is a stimulant. Frequent effects of cocaine usage include inability to sleep, hypervigilance, great excitement, agitation, and motor restlessness. If you are prone toward chronic worry, such effects can only aggravate your mental and emotional state.

ALCOHOL

Avoid Using Alcohol As a Way of Coping with Worry. Alcohol is the opposite of a stimulant, and as such would appear to be an effective way to reduce anxiety. Alcohol, from the pharmacological viewpoint, is a depressant. In the short run it does in fact have the intended effect. It brings quick relief from the aggravation of both nervous tension and the distress associated with a nagging worry.

However, in the long run, a bad bargain is made. The quick relief from an unpleasant emotional state sets up a vicious circle. The quick relief is a form of almost instant *reinforcement*, a psychological payoff that strengthens a habit.

The habit of drinking as a way of coping with worry gets stronger and stronger with repetition. Eventually the habit gets an almost iron grip on behavior and is very difficult to break. This "psychological addiction" is something distinct from the fact that in some persons the regular consumption of alcohol may lead to "physiological addiction," an actual physical need for the drug in question.

Because alcohol is a toxic substance it should be used in moderation, not abused. When it *is* abused, it has a long-run negative impact on the health of neurons in the brain, the cells we think with. Aside from memory loss, one of the signs and symptoms sometimes associated with *alcohol amnestic disorder* is excessive worry over little things. The brain cannot function effectively enough to produce the kind of clear thinking that keeps petty problems in perspective.

THE FEINGOLD HYPOTHESIS

Restrict Foods Containing Artificial Flavors and Colors.
According to the Feingold hypothesis, these foods may
play an important causal role in hyperactive behavior and
attention deficit disorder in children. (Benjamin Feingold
is a pediatrician.) Notice that the word *hypothesis* is used.
Consequently, the central idea advanced is not held by all
mental health workers to be an acceptable one. Nonetheless, the Feingold hypothesis has won enough adherents
that it merits serious attention.

According to the hypothesis, artificial additives in
highly processed foods may produce allergic reactions in
some children. The hypothesis, since its original presentation in the context of clinical pediatric work, has been
extended to include adults. Consequently, it is possible
that at least some adults find themselves restless, agi-
tated, and unnecessarily worried because their central
nervous system is irritated by unwelcome chemicals.

Again, as with the recommendations associated with
avoiding hypoglycemia, the dietary changes you make in
accordance with the hypothesis are healthful ones. As
much as possible, eat fresh foods, not processed ones.
Fresh fruits and vegetables are preferred over canned ones.
Fresh meats and fish are preferred over canned varieties
and processed products, such as most wieners. More and
more manufacturers are controlling artificial additives. So
read the fine print on the back of the labels on cans,
boxes, and packages for ingredients. (For example, some
wieners have few if any artificial ingredients. But you
must *read* the label!)

If the ingredients begin to remind you more of a chemical feast than a food, think twice about purchasing or
eating the item. Fortunately, as already indicated, the situation is improving.

I am well aware that in our present eating environment, with the need to transport food over long distances
and preserve it for extended periods of time, that

chemical preservatives have a proper place. The Feingold hypothesis does not, however, make an issue of most food preservatives. The real problem is the artificial flavors and colors, and these can be spotted readily by reading labels.

Remember that in reading labels the fine print on the back of the label is far more important than the big print on the front. The big print is designed to make an emotional appeal; the small print is provided in order to give you *information*.

No one is advising you to avoid all artificial ingredients. This is almost certainly impractical and nearly impossible. That is why I use the word *restrict* instead of *eliminate*. Do what you can for yourself in a practical way.

You may or may not find restricting artificial flavors and colors to be beneficial. But it is one of those notions that you can readily test for yourself.

MILK

Drink More Milk. Milk has been called "nature's own tranquilizer." We put babies to sleep with a milk bottle. Three-year-old Josephine comes into the house crying. She was pushed by an older child, fell, and scraped her knee. After kissing and comforting her, her mother gives her a cookie and a glass of milk.

A standard home remedy for restlessness or an inability to become drowsy before retiring at night is to drink some milk.

Why has milk acquired this reputation of being something of a tranquilizer? It turns out that milk is very high in an amino acid called *tryptophan*, one of the amino acids associated with protein. It also turns out that tryptophan is an important ingredient in the synthesis of a neurotransmitter, a chemical messenger in the brain, called *serotonin*. There is evidence suggesting that optimal levels of serotonin facilitate mental calm.

In terms of folk medicine, the link between milk and mental calm is well established. But the evidence is merely anecdotal and far from rigorous. It's "just people talking to each other without a scientific basis." In terms of actual research, the link between serotonin and mental calm is far from winning universal consensus. However, in view of the fact that drinking milk is in general thought to be healthful, it may have a place in your arsenal of weapons against chronic worry. In other words, it won't hurt to give it a try and see if drinking milk works for you.

You may be lactose intolerant. Many adults are. If so, be sure you drink milk that is either lactose free or lactose reduced. Such milk is now readily available.

You may object that you can't afford the extra calories. An eight-ounce glass of whole milk contains 160 calories. On the other hand, a four-ounce glass of nonfat milk contains only forty calories. I have found that this is an adequate amount of milk when it is being consumed specifically in order to induce relaxation. Also, nonfat milk is as high in tryptophan as is whole milk.

It should also be noted that milk is high in calcium. There is some possibility that calcium helps to normalize the firing of neurons, the brain's communication cells. And this too may assist in facilitating mental calm.

Having said all of these good things about milk, it is important to note that tryptophan can be found in most protein foods. So if you eat a diet high in animal and dairy products, you are probably getting plenty of tryptophan. Nonetheless, when you feel a little uptight, restless, or worried, you can experiment and find out for yourself if milk helps.

Although tryptophan locked into ordinary foods is desirable, when it is taken as a separate substance it can be harmful. *Do not self-prescribe tryptophan pills.* Excessive amounts of tryptophan taken in this way have been linked to anemia and even death.

Get your tryptophan from milk and other foods, not from pills.

≋≋ ≋≋ ≋≋ ≋≋ ≋≋ ≋≋ ≋≋ ≋≋ ≋≋

Behavioral Chemistry

At the beginning of this chapter the terms *psychosomatic* and *behavioral medicine* were used to identify this chapter's viewpoint. Another descriptive term that can be introduced at this point is *behavioral chemistry*. Behavioral chemistry can be defined as the study of the causal link between biochemical processes in the cells and bloodstream and our thoughts, moods, and actions. It is a large field of study with a lot of potential. To a large extent, the approach taken in this chapter can be thought of as a practical application of behavioral chemistry.

Note that the practical applications and tips given all fall in the category of benign suggestions. They won't do you any harm, and they might do you some good. You can find out by trying the suggestions that appeal to you.

Although it *is* important to get your blood chemistry on an even keel if you want to stop worrying excessively, it is also important to note that optimal blood chemistry is a *necessary* condition to mental health, not a *sufficient* one. In other words, it is a link in the chain, but not the whole chain. In order to complete the whole picture of how to stop worrying we need to turn to *psychological* approaches, approaches that see you as a whole person, as a complex human being with thoughts, habits, and emotions. Future chapters focus on these kinds of approaches.

Key Points to Remember

□⊸   The approach taken in this chapter is based on the assumption that biological processes underlie psychological events.

□⊸   The terms *psychosomatic* and *behavioral medicine* are sometimes used to describe this chapter's viewpoint.

□— The term *hypoglycemia* means "low blood sugar." Practical steps you can take to avoid hypoglycemia include: (1) avoid or restrict dietary sugar, (2) restrict refined carbohydrates, (3) use coffee and drinks containing caffeine in moderation, and (4) increase your intake of complex carbohydrates and proteins.

□— Stimulants are chemical agents that tend to increase central nervous system arousal. Consequently they have an adverse effect on anxiety. Use stimulants in moderation.

□— Alcohol has the capacity to temporarily reduce anxiety. However, its long-run effects are adverse because it is both a toxic and an addictive substance. Avoid using alcohol as a way of coping with worry.

□— The Feingold hypothesis suggests that foods containing artificial flavors and colors may induce restlessness, agitation, and unnecessary worry. Consider restricting your intake of foods containing artificial flavors and colors.

□— Milk has been called "nature's own tranquilizer." Consequently, weigh the value of drinking more milk.

□— Another descriptive term that can be applied to the viewpoint in this chapter is *behavioral chemistry*.

3 OUR EMOTIONAL CONFLICTS: UNDERSTANDING THE INNER STRUGGLE

It is late at night and you are watching a rerun of the old, classic *Honeymooners* series starring Jackie Gleason as Ralph Kramden. Alice has just done something that has irritated Ralph beyond belief. He rants. He raves. He shakes his fist in the air when she is not looking and declares, "One of these days. One of these days!" The implication is that one of these days he will lose his ability to inhibit his actions and give her a sock on the jaw. After a fifteen- or twenty-minute emotional roller coaster ride, Alice and Ralph make up. And he croons, "Alice, you're the greatest!"

You have just witnessed a titanic emotional conflict and its resolution.

Somehow we find this funny.

It's probably because we see ourselves reflected in a distorted and exaggerated way. It's like looking in a funhouse mirror.

Unfortunately, we are all prone to emotional conflicts. It comes with life. It is part of the territory. In this chapter you will gain a greater understanding of how emotional conflicts induce anxiety and irrational worry. And you will be introduced to a set of practical suggestions that are likely to help you reduce the adverse effects of emotional conflicts.

This chapter will help you to understand your inner struggle and ways to cope with it.

The Three Faces of You

In order to understand emotional conflicts it is helpful to think in terms of "the three faces of you." In this presentation I am borrowing straight from classical Freudian theory. Sigmund Freud was born in 1856 and died in 1939. He was one of the most remarkable thinkers of the twentieth century. Although many of his assertions and findings are debatable, his theory of personality is widely regarded as a highly useful one. In order to appreciate some of the practical suggestions that will be made later, it is essential to have some understanding of that theory.

THE PRIMAL SELF

According to Freud, every human being has an inborn id. The *id* can be called the primal self ("first self"). It is present in an infant and it stays with you all of your life. One way to characterize the id is to call it "the inner animal." It is oriented toward pleasure and pleasure alone. It exists only for itself. It is the reservoir of all of your biological drives including hunger, thirst, the need to escape from pain, the need for sleep, sex, and aggressiveness. When an infant cries for milk the id is the causal agent. When an adult is hungry it is still the id that is operating. If your personality were pure id, you would be no better than Frankenstein's monster: a stumbling, psychologically blind creature filled with raw *need*.

THE "I" OF YOUR PERSONALITY

Around the time that you were a toddler and a preschooler the "I" of your personality began to form. This manner of thinking about yourself found its way into your speech patterns. "I want candy!" "I won't do it!" "I

love you." "I hate you." Also, you learned your first name
and began to use it. "I'm Billy." "I'm Susan." "What's
your name?"

The "I" of your personality is called the *ego*. The ego
is what makes reality contact possible. When the ego is
strong, when you have high self-esteem, it helps you to
plan realistically and wait for gratification. It has no needs
of its own. Like a computer that serves the whims of its
operator, the ego essentially exists to serve the whims of
the id.

THE SOCIAL SELF

By the time your were six or seven years old you probably
had formed a social self. You knew that some things were
wrong and that some things were right. You had a concept of either "bad boy" or "bad girl." Conversely, you had
acquired the related concepts of either "good boy" or
"good girl." You knew you had a last name, a family name.
And in most cases you identified with it and thought of
yourself as a member of the family. Also, you may have
acquired religious concepts and values.

The social self is the "we" of the personality. Freud
called it the *superego*. The superego is the source of all
shame and guilt. When you think of deviating from your
early moral training, the superego kicks in and says, "No.
You shouldn't do that!" It tries to stop you, acting like an
inner guard.

Banish the Thought!

We have all heard the phrase, "Banish the thought!"
Scarlett O'Hara, heroine of *Gone with the Wind*, used to
say when she was unhappy with a situation and the
thoughts associated with it, "I'll think about that tomorrow." She tried voluntarily to banish unwelcome
thoughts. This approach to mental censorship is called

suppression. By the way, it doesn't work very well. It is hard to force a thought out of the mind by an act of will. If you don't believe me, try off and on today to *not* think of a white elephant.

The mind has developed another way of dealing with unwelcome thoughts. Freud called it *repression*. Repression acts like an invisible hand in the mind, shoving unwelcome thoughts into a psychological nether world that exists at an unconscious level. Unlike suppression, repression is involuntary. It doesn't require an act of will. It just happens. Think of the unconscious domain as a kind of psychological Siberia. Ideas and wishes sent to psychological Siberia are supposed to be gone forever. But they're not. They're not dead, and they have a way of returning and causing emotional trouble. Freud called this *the return of the repressed*.

What thoughts are banished to the unconscious level? The three principal categories are: (1) emotionally painful childhood experiences, (2) forbidden sexual wishes, and (3) forbidden aggressive wishes. Classical psychoanalysis, as a form of therapy, was concerned with uncovering these repressed elements and bringing them under conscious, rational control.

Why You Worry

Freud's theory of personality gives us one answer to the question: "Why do you worry so much?" In the context of this question, I am assuming that the worry is both irrational and excessive. It is the kind of chronic worry described in Chapter 1, the kind of worry that is the central concern of this book.

Let's go back to Ralph Kramden who has the fantasy that he may hit Alice "one of these days." Now let's think about a real life Ralph Kramden, and add a new dimension to his personality. Let's call him Ralph II to distinguish him from the television Ralph. He feels hostile toward his wife, but he *feels guilty about it*. He represses his hostility, banishes it to the unconscious level. He buys her flowers on her birthday, arranges special treats, trying somewhat in vain to prove to himself how much he loves her. Ralph II is an oversocialized person. He tries too hard to be a nice guy. He feels used and abused by his wife. Although he is, of course, faintly aware of twitches of hostility, he is not aware of the fact that his anger flows at a very deep psychological level.

One day while Ralph II is driving the bus he begins to wonder what would happen if a front tire blew out. He wonders how he would cope in an emergency. An involuntary mental movie plays itself in which he sees the bus going out of control, a pedestrian being run over, passengers badly injured when the bus jumps the curve and hits a building. All of this worry is irrational, unbidden, and seems to come from nowhere.

I say it *seems* to come from nowhere. Actually, remember that Ralph II has a lot of repressed hostility toward his wife. There *is* in a sense a realistic fear present. It is the fear that he will act out his hostility and injure his wife. This fear comes from the fact that he's threatened by the possibility that his ego won't be able to hold back his forbidden wish. This emotional conflict, chaotic and not understood at all, produces what Freud called "neurotic anxiety." In short, neurotic anxiety arises from the fear that one might in fact put a repressed wish into action.

But the wish *is* repressed. Therefore it expresses itself in distorted form. An ego defense mechanism called *projection* kicks in. A projection takes place when an unconscious psychological element is perceived as arising from an external source. Consequently, Ralph II projects his neurotic anxiety onto the external world: the tires might blow out and a series of disasters might follow. The nebulous cloud of anxiety that has been floating over his head, arising from his doubts about his own self-control, is condensed into what appears to be an objective reality.

≋≋ ≋≋ ≋≋ ≋≋ ≋≋ ≋≋ ≋≋ ≋≋ ≋≋

I know all of this sounds somewhat incredible. It sounds incredible because it is irrational, which is another way of saying that it's illogical. However, remember that neurotic anxiety, excessive worry in which psychological molehills are made into psychological mountains, *is* irrational. If the explanation sounds a bit convoluted it is because psychodynamic theory suggests that the unconscious domain is a sort of Alice in Wonderland world that makes a mockery of common sense.

Actually, a repressed wish is at the core of many irrational fears. One of my clients, Gale W., was a woman who suffered from a fairly severe case of *agoraphobia*, a condition characterized by a fear of straying very far from home. What was the repressed wish that explained her phobia? She was disgusted with her husband, who was a bore, mistreated her, discounted her, and gave her almost no affection. Gale was an intelligent woman, quite a talented artist. She was also a highly traditional woman who yearned to be a responsible wife and mother. Her traditional role, associated with her superego, conflicted with her repressed wish to simply *leave*, to get out of the marriage that at the most profound level of her personality she perceived to be a very bad bargain indeed. But she couldn't admit her wish honestly to herself. So the repressed content expressed itself in symbolic form, a kind of sign language: agoraphobia. The *conscious* fear of leaving home was a way of containing the *unconscious* wish to take flight.

The Anatomy of Emotional Conflict

It will help you cope with emotional conflict if you can get a clear picture of its categories. When you are troubled and worried you will be able to label the *kind* of conflict you are in, and this will help to set you free. Three fundamental kinds of conflict will be identified.

THE APPROACH-APPROACH CONFLICT

An approach-approach conflict exists when you have two or more good choices, but can't select readily between them. A mild example is trying to decide which of two birthday cards to buy. An intense example that certainly would involve emotional turmoil is trying to decide which of two people you really love and want to marry. An old movie starring Ginger Rogers called *Tom, Dick, and Harry* had her in a situation where she could take her pick of any one of three nice guys. The entire plot, a light romantic comedy, arises from her mental and emotional turmoil as she approaches her final choice.

THE APPROACH-AVOIDANCE CONFLICT

An approach-avoidance conflict exists when a "goal" in your psychological world has both positive and negative features. An everyday example is the decision to order or not to order a piece of pie with lunch. On the positive side, you *want* the sweetness of the pie, the feeling of the crust in your mouth, and the tartness of the apples. But you *don't want* the calories and the extra fat it will put on you. So you go back and forth for a while before you say yes or no to yourself.

A more intense version of an approach-avoidance conflict was already given with the case of Gale W. On the positive side, she wished to approach the goal of personal freedom because it meant no longer being taken for granted; it also included the possibility of someday finding a meaningful relationship. On the negative side, in terms of her superego, attainment of the goal signified irresponsibility and the abandonment of her traditional values.

THE AVOIDANCE-AVOIDANCE CONFLICT

An avoidance-avoidance conflict exists when your psychological world contains two negative goals. (The word *goal* in motivational psychology is correctly used in both positive and negative terms.) A mild example of an avoidance-avoidance conflict is given when a child is told by a parent to make a choice between one of two chores: washing the dinner dishes or sweeping the porch and throwing out the garbage. The child sees both choices in negative terms, and would like to avoid both, although this is, of course, impossible.

Here is an example of an avoidance-avoidance conflict with a high emotional charge, one capable of producing plenty of worry. A surgeon has just told Grace D. that she has cancer of the colon and that an operation might give her a chance for life. The surgery will be quite radical and she will have to have follow-up chemotherapy. Grace is panic-stricken and would like to avoid surgery at all costs. But what *is* the cost of avoiding surgery? The surgeon assures her that if she avoids surgery she will almost certainly die a painful death in the near future. Grace also wants to avoid death. Perhaps you feel that the choice is not so difficult after all. You would choose surgery. Perhaps. But not all people make this choice. The point is that if Grace is sure which way she wants to go, there is little or no emotional conflict. But if she has ideas that make her feel both choices are nearly unacceptable, then she will be filled with worry until she makes a firm decision. (Such a decision will not, of course dispel all worry, because any choice retains seriously worrisome elements.)

An avoidance-avoidance conflict presents us with a choice between two evils. It is a question of jumping out of the frying pan into the fire. Such a conflict is a double bind, a no-win situation. And, as such, can be a source of great emotional distress.

Ending the Civil War with Yourself

The kind of emotional conflict described in this chapter may be likened to a civil war, in this case a civil war within yourself. You are in a state of conflict because, in psychoanalytical terms, your id is often at war with your superego. The two are sometimes engaged in a titanic struggle. The ego must act something like the United Nations. If the ego is weak when it interferes, the situation can get worse. If the ego is strong, informed, and confident, it can make the situation better. The coping strategies listed below are all designed to add both strength and information to your ego. And they will help you end the civil war within yourself. This in turn will have the beneficial effect of reducing your general level of worry.

KEEPING A JOURNAL

Keep a Journal of Your Thoughts. A journal of your thoughts includes reflections, general observations, emotional states, and so forth. Such a journal is a psychological-emotional journal. It is not a diary of objective events, of weddings you went to and other actual events of your life. On the contrary, it is a record of your *inner world*, the world we all live of fantasy and perception. You may of course wish to make dated entries in order to have a running record of your psychological development.

You don't have to feel compelled to make regular, daily entries. But when the spirit moves you, when the impulse strikes, jot down, without regard to style, your thoughts about situations, other people, an emotional crisis you are going through, and so forth. What is the value of this activity?

There are two principal values. First, examining your thoughts in writing will help you develop *insight* into your emotional conflicts. *Insight* is a kind of self-understanding in which you bring together discon-nected thoughts into a meaningful whole. You perceive the deeper aspects of your problem, its psychological roots. Although it is now acknowledged in the field of psychotherapy that insight frequently is not enough to bring about significant behavioral change, it is also a point worth making that insight can often be *useful*. Insight is often an important first step in the direction of actually taking *effective action*, which is, of course, far more important than insight itself.

Second, examining your thoughts in writing will help you to develop *cognitive control*, a kind of self-mastery of your thoughts. Chaotic ideas and blind impulses at the unconscious level often control you, you don't control them. It is much like the situation of the tail wagging the dog instead of the dog wagging the tail. You want to gain conscious control of your hidden emotions so that you will not be at the mercy of the anxiety and worry that they cause.

FORBIDDEN WISHES

Look for the Forbidden Wish at the Core of an Irrational Fear. Luther N. suffers from *hypochondriasis*, irrational worry about his health. He has a headache, and thinks he might have a brain tumor. He gets a pain in his stomach, and thinks he might have inflammatory bowel syndrome. He gets a pain in his chest, and he thinks that he might be having a heart attack. He worries constantly about his health, and spends a small fortune on over-the-counter medicines. He is disgusted with physicians because in the end they all tell him that there is "nothing wrong with you," and he *knows* that there is. At the core of Luther's hypochondriasis there lurks a forbidden wish. It is an awful wish. It is the wish to destroy himself. He attempted suicide twice when he was younger—once when he was a teenager and once when he was twenty-three. Now, married and a financially successful certified public accountant, at age thirty-three he still has repressed self-destructive tendencies. One of the ways of protecting himself against himself is to be consciously preoccupied with his health.

Is a forbidden wish at the core of every irrational fear and unfounded worry? No, of course not. Common sense alone tells us that this can't be so. Let's return to the problem of hypochondriasis with a different case. There was a famous movie star who took over sixty vitamin pills a day for a number of years as he approached old age. He had a wish all right, but it wasn't a forbidden one. His egotistic nature demanded of life that he remain handsome and young forever. He had an unreasonable fear of aging and losing his good looks. Taking the pills was the magic ritual that was supposed to keep the worst from happening. At the core of some irrational fears is an *impossible wish*, not an forbidden one.

However, this chapter, unlike future chapters, is about the role that emotional *conflict* plays in worry. The actor was not in a state of conflict. He was simply an arrogant, superficial person with a selfish streak. However, when a person is in a state of conflict like Luther or Joanna, when there is an inner civil war, then there often exists a forbidden wish.

Assume for the moment that there is a forbidden wish at the core of an irrational fear that you have, a fear that induces excessive worry. Identifying and recognizing the wish can help you eventually free yourself from its negative influence.

SUBLIMATION

Use Sublimation. Sublimation is an ego defense mechanism in which the psychological energy associated with unacceptable impulses is redirected into more acceptable form. Raymond Chandler is the author of *The Big Sleep* and other novels featuring the adventures of Philip Marlowe, an extraordinary private investigator. Chandler was a troubled man. He was overcontrolled by his mother, highly submissive to her, and certainly had a lot of emotional conflict surrounding both his sexual life and his aggressive impulses. He didn't marry until his mother died, and then his wife was nineteen years older than he was. One of the ways that Chandler kept himself relatively stable and functioning effectively for years was by discharging his emotional conflict through the medium of his books. Writing out his worst fears in fictional form helped him to reduce the general level of anxiety and worry in his daily life. The fictional Philip Marlowe treats bad women badly, good women like queens, and punishes villains when necessary.

Write or draw or paint for yourself. Use your imagination and let your strong emotions out on paper. The activity is harmless; it can hurt no one. It is also constructive; it allows you to see your mixed up feelings in concrete form. Unacceptable energy is discharged and drained away, making you *less* likely actually to do something that you will regret. This means that you will be able to worry less about yourself and what you might do if you lose self-control.

NOVELS AND MOVIES

Use Novels and Movies As a Means of Discharging Unacceptable Sexual and Aggressive Impulses. It would seem to be unnecessary to give this advice because novels and movies are both so popular. Nevertheless, there are a couple of worthwhile points to be made. The advice given in this section is very similar to the advice about using sublimation. Fantasy, like sublimation, is an ego defense mechanism. Both allow for the harmless discharge of potentially damaging psychological energy. The use of sublimation is the more effective of the two mechanisms because it is *active*, not passive. In a commercial fantasy, you are the member of an audience. Someone else creates the fantasy for you. In sublimation, you are the author of the fantasy, and it is tailor-made for your personality.

Having noted that commercial fantasy is more passive than sublimation, let us now note that reading a novel involves a higher level of cognitive involvement than does watching a movie. When you read a novel you have to think, visualize, and use your imagination in order to create the world into which you are temporarily escaping. This can be very beneficial for your mental health, much more so than watching movies. The media philosopher Marshall McLuhan said that the printed word is a "hot" medium and that television is a "cool" medium. The word *hot* was chosen to suggest psychological and emotional involvement. Obviously, if the medium is "hot" it will be more effective in draining off unwanted impulses than if it is "cool."

If you were once in the habit of reading novels, and the habit has dropped away, consider reinstating it.

COMPROMISE

Learn to Make Compromises with Yourself. Ernest Jones, psychoanalyst and Freud's principal biographer, said, "The art of living is the art of compromise." In the context of this chapter, this means that you need to find a way to negotiate some kind of a truce between your warring feelings. Again, using the example of the ego functioning somewhat like the United Nations, it has to try to act as a peacekeeper. It has to be aware of the impulses arising from the id and the unconscious domain, impulses that are forbidden in terms of your moral code. And it has to be aware of the prohibitions and restrictions of your superego. If these are resolved to some degree, even if not completely, you will experience greater peace of mind. In turn, you will suffer less from compulsive worry.

Here is a practical example of the compromise principal. Abigail D., a sweet, self-effacing bank teller who is thirty-three and lives alone, is dominated by an unfeeling, authoritarian supervisor. Her id would like to sock the supervisor in the jaw and teach her a lesson. Abigail's superego is horrified by the idea. "Nice" women don't go

around socking supervisors. Aware of her hostility, Abigail buys a punch toy and sets it up in a spare bedroom. When she comes home from work she blows off steam by hitting the punch toy and pretending that it is her supervisor. Abigail admits her hostility to herself and has a lot of fun hitting the punch toy. The activity seems childish, and of course, it *is*. However, that is to some extent the point. Her ego, the psychological referee, allows the emotional regression in service of the id. Although this compromise between her id and her ego is far from completely satisfactory, it helps her to adapt to an adverse working situation. Abigail used to worry that she would say something that she would regret to her supervisor. But now she feels much more in control in the other's presence.

KIND OF CONFLICT

Identify the Kind of Conflict Situation You Are In. Recall that the three kinds of conflict situations are: (1) approach-approach, (2) approach-avoidance, and (3) avoidance-avoidance. Take a realistic look at the motivational forces that are tugging at you and attach a conscious label to what you are going through. (Review the section called "The Anatomy of Emotional Conflict" for help.)

Sheila R. said to herself, "I'm in an approach-avoidance conflict over my relationship with Sam." When she reached this conclusion she said to herself, "Well, I can't have my cake and eat it too. I've got to marry Sam or go on to someone else. Otherwise I'll go in circles forever." Sheila made a first list *in writing* of Sam's positive qualities (the characteristics in him that elicited approach). Then she made a second list of his negative qualities (the characteristics in him that elicited avoidance). She worked on the list off and on for several days, carrying it in her purse. The labeling of the conflict and its associated analysis helped her finally to resolve her dilemma, and she was able to banish the worry associated with it.

SELF-ACCEPTANCE

Practice Greater Self-Acceptance. Compulsive worriers tend to be too self-critical. They set high standards for themselves. They tend often to have a perfectionistic streak. And when they fail to meet rigid personal criteria, they are disgusted with themselves. They don't want to have ugly sexual and aggressive impulses. They want to deny their psychological reality. But *we all have them*. It's just a part of human nature. The trick is to realize that they can't be destroyed. Consequently, they must be managed. Self-acceptance says, "I love me *with* my faults. I care about myself in spite of my shortcomings. I forgive myself for being human."

Breaking the Psychological Chain

In this chapter I have shown you how our emotional conflicts are related in a kind of psychological chain originating with ideas at an unconscious mental level leading eventually to conscious worry. I have offered practical ways of breaking one of the strongest links in the chain, the link of *repression*, the link that makes us the victim of forbidden impulses. By applying the suggestions made in this chapter you really can diminish the level of chronic worry in your life.

Key Points to Remember

□⚊ We are all prone to emotional conflicts.

□⚊ Emotional conflicts often induce anxiety and irrational worry.

□⚊ The "three faces of you" are your primal self, the "I" of your personality, and your social self. Freud called these the *id*, *ego*, and *superego*.

□⚊ *Suppression* is the effort to banish an unwelcome thought by an act of will. *Repression* is an involuntary process that shoves unwelcome thoughts into a psychological nether world that exists at an unconscious level.

□⚊ One source of anxiety and worry is the fear that repressed wishes will break out of their prison, and that consequently we will act out our worst forbidden impulses.

▫▬ An approach-approach conflict exists when you have two or more good choices, but can't select readily between them.

▫▬ An approach-avoidance conflict exists when a "goal" in your psychological world has both positive and negative features.

▫▬ An avoidance-avoidance conflict exists when your psychological world contains two negative goals.

▫▬ Keep a journal of your thoughts.

▫▬ Look for the forbidden wish at the core of an irrational fear.

▫▬ Use sublimation as a way of redirecting unacceptable impulses into a more acceptable form.

▫▬ Use novels and movies as a means of discharging unacceptable sexual and aggressive impulses.

▫▬ Learn to make compromises with yourself.

▫▬ Identify the kind of conflict situation you are in.

▫▬ Practice greater self-acceptance.

4 THE WORRY HABIT: WHAT HAS BEEN LEARNED CAN BE UNLEARNED

You are a chronic worrier.

Saying that you *are* a chronic worrier suggests that it is part of your very being, a part of your individual nature.

Perhaps you even say, "I guess I'm just a born worrywart."

But you're wrong.

Repeat. You're *wrong*.

You weren't born a worrywart. There is nothing innate about a tendency toward compulsive worry. On the contrary, the behavior is learned. It's a *habit*, a cluster of related learned responses. And what has been learned can be unlearned.

This chapter will specify the main ways in which the worry habit is acquired. And it will also specify practical strategies for unmaking its cluster of maladaptive responses.

Brent M. is a forty-four-year-old tax attorney. He is married to Abigail, and is the father of three children. The family lives in a comfortable paid-for home in the suburbs. The home is paid for because for a number of years Brent insisted on putting every spare dollar into retiring the original loan against the house. The furniture is threadbare. Abigail and the children make do with a very limited, inexpensive wardrobe. Brent drives an up-to-date car and has a nicely decorated office. But this is because necessity demands that he maintain a good business front.

Actually Brent is a sort of reincarnation of Old Scrooge, the miser. Except for one reliable employee, he uses all part-time help. He encourages his wife to serve cheap cuts of meat, and they seldom eat out even at a family restaurant. Why is Brent so stingy? Because he is worried about money. He worries constantly that he will go bankrupt. Sometimes he wakes up in the middle of the night in a cold sweat. He's just had a nightmare, and in it he was a homeless old man. His heart is pounding and he is covered with perspiration. His worry about money is highly unrealistic. Not only is his house paid for, he has $50,000 invested in an annuity, $100,000 in U.S. Treasury bills, and about $25,000 cash in a checking and savings account.

I've already said that Brent is stingy because he is worried about money. But let's probe more deeply. Why does he worry so much about money?

Brent's father was an alcoholic, an irresponsible, lovable man with a warm personality. Everybody loved "good old Oscar." But good old Oscar held a series of unreliable jobs and was a victim of pathological gambling. Brent remembers three evictions in his childhood. He vividly recalls standing on the sidewalk when he was eight years old with his father, mother, and sister. The had just been ejected from an apartment, the family furniture was piled up in public view, and they had nowhere to go. They were helped out of their crisis by a charitable organization.

Brent's sad experiences in childhood associated with the mismanagement of money made an indelible impression on him. As a young man going to school, he vowed that he would never suffer the same fate that his father had suffered. That is why he became a tax attorney. He wanted to be money's master, not the other way around. In the beginning, worrying about money was, in a sense, functional. It led to a paid-for home and financial security. But now worry has become a habit, a bad habit. What was once adaptive, is now maladaptive. And the worry habit is interfering with the quality of his life. His wife, for one, feels deprived of some of the nicer things her sisters and friends have, and she is bitter about it. The children complain that the family has never had a real vacation. Obviously, it would presently be to Brent's advantage to get over the worry habit and his miserly ways.

But a habit like Brent's can't be unmade by willpower. He can't just say to himself, "I'll quit this habit. It's no longer serving any purpose. It's useless." If the habit is compulsive, which Brent's is, then it asserts itself in spite of his will and the fact that he recognizes it to be irrational.

A habit has *strength*. However, it can be weakened. Before we can devise ways to unmake the worry habit, we need to understand the learning process that underlies it.

Ways the Worry Habit Is Learned

Let's try a word association test. I say *thunder*. What do you say? If you're not trying to tease me and show me that maybe I don't know what I'm doing, you probably say *lightning*. (Even if you don't *say* it, I'll bet you *thought* it.) The word *mom* makes us think of *dad*. *Bread* makes us think of *butter*. And so forth. The process of *association*, the linking together of ideas, is the first way in which the worry habit is learned.

BELLS ARE RINGING

The great Russian physiologist Ivan Pavlov did his research at the University of Moscow in the early part of this century. His subjects were dogs. He found that if you rang a bell and immediately followed the ringing with food, the dog would learn to salivate to the bell alone.

He called such salivation a *psychological secretion* or *conditional reflex*, because the reflex that was normally elicited by food in the mouth became conditional on the sounding of a bell. (Actually Pavlov didn't really ring a bell. He used a pure tone, more like a beep. As a consequence, he could vary the pitch and amplitude. The term *bell* has become the popular one, and I'll use it for convenience, but put mental quotes around it. Also, Pavlov's original term *conditional reflex* is usually referred to in the United States as a *conditioned reflex*. From here on out I'll use this term.)

What has a dog trained by Pavlov learned? It has learned an association. The bell is associated with food. Hearing the bell, it expects to be fed. In a word, the bell has become a *signal*, a stimulus that "predicts" the future. Something like this is what happens to you when you develop a learned fear. Bells are ringing, so to speak, and they elicit anxiety. (Note that anxiety and worry are always future oriented. They refer to something that *might* happen.)

A powerful example of how a fear is learned in a human being is given by the pioneering research of Rosalie Raynor, an experimental psychologist, and John B. Watson, the father of behaviorism. Raynor, who did the actual experimental work, showed a white rat to a preschool child named Albert. She adapted Albert to the rat. He was able to handle it and showed no fear of it. Then one day while Albert was stroking the rat in the laboratory Rosalie sounded a loud gong behind Albert. Startled, Albert dropped the white rat and began to cry. The next time that Albert was brought into the laboratory and saw the white rat he began to whimper and pull away. (It is easy to see that if Albert were to be taken to the laboratory on future days he would worry about what was going to happen when he arrived while he was making the trip.) The loud gong is like the Pavlovian bell; crying is the conditioned reflex. *Fear*, in this case, is a conditioned emotional reaction.

Raynor was able to show that Albert was also afraid of things that were in any way similar to the white rat. Albert was afraid of a Santa Claus mask because it had a white beard, which is reminiscent of white fur. He was afraid of a white terry-cloth dish towel rolled up into a ball. The term used to describe the conditioned emotional reaction to objects similar to the original feared stimulus is *anxiety*. Learned anxiety is often at the core of much chronic worry.

Raynor had devised methods of deconditioning Albert. However, Albert's mother, somewhat distressed by the course of Raynor and Watson's research, removed the child before the experimental work was complete. Today an experiment such as the Raynor-Watson one would not be conducted; it is considered unethical because it is certainly not in the best long-term interests of the child.

However, life itself has a cruel way of sometimes creating situations that resemble the artificial circumstances of the laboratory. Douglas G. choked on a fish bone when he was a six-year-old child. The bone wedged in his trachea and had to be removed by a physician in an emergency room. The whole experience was extremely traumatic, and Douglas, now thirty-three, still remembers it well. Today when he eats fish, even a boneless filet, he begins to worry about choking. He eats it carefully, taking small bites and chewing each bite many times, constantly checking with his tongue for a bone. Often he simply refuses fish. Once, in the early days of his marriage, his wife told him that she was planning to have fish for dinner. He worried about dinner and the possibility that he might choke all day. For Douglas, the sight of fish on a plate is like the white rat for Albert. The childhood choking incident was like the loud gong. An association has been formed. Fish, for Douglas, is a bell that rings the related emotional responses of fear, anxiety, and worry.

Let's return to the case of Brent M., the tax attorney. The traumatic experience of being evicted and standing on the sidewalk with the family furniture is like the loud gong for Albert. The lack of money, real or anticipated, is like the white rat, the warning signal.

As you can see, many fears are conditioned emotional reactions acquired between a cue with signal value and a bad experience.

THE AVOIDANCE SYNDROME

Mark Twain said he once had a cat who was burned by a hot stove. He noted that a peculiarity of the cat's behavior was that it was afraid not only of hot stoves, but of *cold* stoves too. Placed on a cold stove, the cat immediately jumped off. The cat was showing an avoidance reaction.

A somewhat more formal presentation of what Mark Twain observed can be obtained by considering avoidance conditioning experiments with monkeys. I am going to present a typical experiment because it will help you to understand clearly the underlying learning process involved in habitual worry. In essence, we're going to create a laboratory neurosis in a monkey. (The following description is based on actual research conducted by Joseph V. Brady.)

One of the monkeys is the executive monkey. The second monkey is the control monkey. For convenience, let's give each one of them a name. The executive monkey will be Eugene and the control monkey will be Conrad. They are sitting next to each other, trapped in yoked chairs. Both receive somewhat painful electric shocks to their feet. At first the shocks are random and unpredictable. Then Eugene is presented with a light and a button. When the light comes on he has 20 seconds to push it. If he manages to do so, neither he nor Conrad will be shocked. It doesn't take long before one of them develops bleeding ulcers. If the experiment is not stopped, the animal may bleed to death.

Before you read on, try to take a guess. Which monkey develops the ulcers? Take a moment to think about it. All right. Got your answer?

It's Eugene, the one who has to make all of the decisions. In my psychology classes, many students guess Conrad because he is helpless and has to go along with Eugene's decisions. However, look at it this way. Eugene becomes an efficient "executive." He almost always stops both of them from getting shocked. The warning light allows Eugene to act in such a way as to *avoid* shock.

Then why does Eugene get an ulcer? It is from the anxiety he suffers when he is actually *in* the situation. When he's "working" he's competent and fairly calm. Information gathered by Brady demonstrated that Eugene's gastric secretions were highest *before* he was in the situation, when he *anticipated* the burden he would be carrying. The secretion of excessive stomach acid is what caused the ulcers. Although Eugene was competent, he was, of course, *worrying*. And, like many who worry, he really had nothing to worry about.

Let's say that we disconnect the shock apparatus. Even if Eugene fouls up now and then, neither he nor Conrad will get shocked. Will Eugene get lazier and lazier and careless? Will he lose his vigilance. The answer is no. He's not about to wait around and find out if the shock is off. He's going to make *sure* to press the button. Pressing the button becomes its own psychological reward because every time that Eugene presses it he experiences *reduction of anxiety*. And so the behavior is self-reinforcing, a kind of psychological perpetual motion.

Again, let's return to Brent's hypervigilant behavior concerning the management of money. His excessive thrift and miserly ways are like Eugene pressing the button. Every time that Brent pinches a dollar he is saving himself from possible dispossession or bankruptcy.

This is why the neurotic process underlying worry does not just wither away with the passage of time. It keeps restrengthening itself. The only way to get over the worry habit is to *consciously* and *actively* work against it, to use the kinds of suggestions made later in this chapter as well as elsewhere in the book.

WHO'S A COPYCAT?

Do you remember when you were a child and you acted somewhat like an older child on the playground, one you really admired? Perhaps you began to imitate the older child's walk or speech patterns. Much to your dismay other kids your own age called, "Copycat! Copycat!" in laughter and derision. You felt embarrassed, as if there were something wrong with you.

Well, here's a secret that's not a secret. We're all copycats, because we all assimilate behavior patterns by watching others and taking many of our cues from them. It's a process called *observational learning.*

Sally C.'s mother, Pamela, made herself a victim of chronic worry. As Sally was growing up, she witnessed almost daily a mother who worried about gaining weight and growing old. Pamela was always counting calories and somewhat phobic about food. Food was the enemy that might make her fat. She wasn't anorexic, but she was a compulsive dieter. Pamela worried that her husband didn't love her, and often expressed her fears to Sally. She worried that the house wasn't clean enough when she had company, and imagined that if a sink in a bathroom wasn't spick and span that she would be severely criticized behind her back by friends and relatives.

Now Sally is herself married and the mother of a daughter. And, you guessed it, she too worries about her weight and the condition of the house. Pamela's ways rubbed off on Sally. Worry is, like an airborne virus, contagious. We're all suggestible to some extent, some of us more than others. If you're even moderately suggestible, you can "catch" the worry habit from parents who worry too much through the process of observational learning.

It is quite likely that Brent M.'s three children will become adults who worry about money.

But you protest, "What about the rebel? What about the child who goes against all of the family's ways?" If father shaved every day, the son grows a beard. If mother kept a neat house, the daughter has a house that is disorganized. If father was a compulsive worker, the son is lazy. If mother was a good cook, the daughter eats out at fast food restaurants.

The rebel is certainly not free of observational learning. He or she has observed very well, and is often doing, point for point, the exact opposite of what a parent did.

If the rebellious behavior revolves around a parent's irrational fears and compulsive worries, then the behavior is called *counterphobic*, a kind of behavior designed to repress a fear. The rebel is worried too, but in a kind of reverse way. The rebel is trying to prove, compulsively, that there is nothing to worry about.Consequently, it is quite possible that one of Brent M.'s children will become a spendthrift, wasting money and actually experiencing financial ruin in order to "prove" that Dad was wrong in some way. This is the phenomenon of the *prodigal child*. Interestingly, in a family of several children, it is typical for only one child to be prodigal. In a family where there are no siblings, the individual child will usually not be prodigal.

Unmaking the Worry Habit

Habits, as you have seen, are acquired by a learning process. You can fight fire with fire. The learning process can be turned on itself when the learning has adverse consequences. New, positive learnings can be made to replace old, negative ones. Maladaptive learned responses can be extinguished or modified. There are arts and skills in the *self-modification of behavior*. Some applications of these arts and skills are described below.

SYSTEMATIC DESENSITIZATION

Practice Voluntary Systematic Desensitization. The concept of desensitization is based on the well-known phenomenon of adaptation. We get used to a stimulus or a situation. We adapt to it and it loses its novelty. If an irrelevant buzzer is sounded, an infant's heartbeat will increase, demonstrating attention and, perhaps, the vigilance associated with anxiety. If the buzzer is sounded on a regular basis every five minutes, without a change in pitch or loudness, there will be a gradual decrease in intensity of the response until after several presentations there is no response at all. On a somewhat more complex scale, medical students who in their first year of clinical work find their flesh crawling at the sight of blood, find that in their second or third year they are totally without emotional response to the sight of blood.

This principle of adaptation can be turned to your psychological advantage in your efforts to cope with worry. Let's go back to Brent M., the tax attorney with Scrooge-like traits. He will not allow himself to "waste money." Let's assume that Brent is motivated to get over his irrational fear of expenditures and the worry that goes with his fear. His tightwad ways are causing problems in living, particularly with his wife, who, as was earlier noted, feels deprived.

Systematic desensitization is a step-by-step method of mastering almost any irrational or useless fear. It was developed by the psychiatrist Joseph Wolpe as a technique in psychotherapy. However, it can be adapted as a self-directed coping method.

Here are the instructions:

Step 1. Draw up either mentally or on paper a hierarchy of fearful stimuli or situations associated with a particular problem. The list should start with "weak" stimuli and proceed toward "strong" ones. Each item on the list should be capable of eliciting anxiety.

Step 2. Sit in a comfortable chair and induce a state of relaxation. (See chapter 5 for methods of doing this.) Research conducted by Wolpe suggests that muscular relaxation is incompatible with anxiety. It is antagonistic to it. When relaxation is introduced in the presence of anxiety a phenomenon called *counterconditioning* comes into play, and extinguishes the "blaze" of anxiety.

Step 3. Close your eyes and induce a voluntary fantasy, something like a mental movie with sound and pictures, of the weakest item on the list. For example, Brent might imagine leaving a 20 percent tip in an expensive restaurant. Let's say even this "weak" situation induces an increase in pulse and sweating palms. If so, Brent should reintroduce a relaxation strategy until the anxiety subsides. Then he should again induce the fantasy until he adapts to it, until it no longer elicits anxiety. He then proceeds to the next item on the list, and so forth, until he can tolerate the strongest item without anxiety (paying for a new roof on the house, for example). Each fantasy should have an ending with a pleasant, successful outcome.

The desensitization sessions should be fifteen to twenty minutes in duration. Time should be set aside for them, allowing for about three per week. It might take several weeks before the strongest fantasy can be tolerated without anxiety. When this is finally accomplished, believe it or not, much, if not all, of an irrational fear will be gone.

Perhaps you protest, "But this is a *fantasy*! It's not real life." Well, first let me point out that victims of chronic worry tend to have overactive imaginations. They think obsessively about the worst, about what *might* happen. And what is this but a fantasy? They are *afraid of fantasies.* Systematic desensitization is very logical. It fights fire with fire. It turns voluntary positive fantasies against negative involuntary ones.

Second, fantasy desensitization is used as an antecedent preparation for *in vivo* desensitization, desensitization in real life. *In vivo* desensitization calls for taking small steps, not biting off more than you can chew, and exposing yourself to actual situations that elicit anxiety. Incidentally, this is why the kind of desensitization being described is called "systematic." In both fantasy and *in vivo* desensitization, situations are faced in a planned, orderly fashion based on their rank order. Again, you proceed from "weak" stimuli to "strong" ones.

Systematic desensitization can be used to combat virtually any irrational fear or useless worry. Research has revealed that it is one of the most effective and reliable methods available in psychotherapy.

DISCONNECTING IDEAS

Voluntarily Work on Disconnecting Adversely Associated Ideas. As has been shown, many of our fears are based on the adverse association of ideas. Albert associates the idea of the white rat with the idea of the gong. Brent M. associates the idea of having fun and spending money with winding up homeless on the street. Douglas G. associates eating fish with choking.

One of the things you can and should do when two ideas are connected in an adverse manner is to work on disconnecting them. This requires an act of will. You need to say to yourself, "This connection is a chance connection. It has no real meaning. It is not cause and effect as I seem to think, but a conditioned response. Such a response is involuntary and a kind of nonthink."

COUNTERCONDITIONING

Use Counterconditioning. The trick of using counterconditioning is to associate a feared or negative stimulus with a positive one that naturally arouses a relaxed feeling. The use of counterconditioning as a factor in systematic desensitization was described earlier. But you can use it in almost any situation.

Genevieve R.'s preschool son, Michael, did not want to eat broccoli. The sight of it on his plate elicited spontaneous looks of disgust. Instead of forcing Michael to eat broccoli she knew that he liked a processed cheese product called Cheese Whiz. She asked Michael if he would like some Cheese Whiz with his broccoli. He said that he would like the Cheese Whiz, but no broccoli. She promised him that a single piece of broccoli would be covered with as much Cheese Whiz as he wanted if he would agree to eat the broccoli under these conditions. Michael reluctantly agreed. He ate a small piece of broccoli covered with about two tablespoons of Cheese Whiz. The counterconditioning procedure was instituted each time the family had broccoli for dinner. By the seventh or eighth time broccoli was served almost no Cheese Whiz was required, and Michael ate several pieces of broccoli. Today, as an adult, he enjoys broccoli and other vegetables. Genevieve intelligently used counterconditioning to extinguish the adverse reactions to the broccoli stimulus.

You can do something similar with yourself. Ralph G., who has an adverse reaction to fish on his plate, likes french fries. In a family restaurant, he can use counterconditioning by eating a small amount of fish and a big order of fries. Brent M., who hates to part with money, likes to listen to classical music. He can play tapes that set him at ease when writing checks for household bills.

Peggy E. is taking a statistics course required for a vocational goal she is pursuing. Unfortunately, she suffers from quite a bit of math anxiety and worries a lot about tests. Just picking up the statistics book and looking at formulas for the standard deviation involving square roots and new concepts like "degrees of freedom" is enough to speed up her pulse. Peggy has a particular pair of pajamas and an old blue bathrobe that make her feel cozy and secure. She decides to put them on before she does her math homework. Studying in her "security clothes" helps her relax and concentrate.

NONAVOIDANCE

Practice Voluntary Nonavoidance. When you are in the presence of a stimulus or a situation that makes you anxious, the natural tendency is to avoid. When Eugene, the executive monkey, was presented with a light and a button that allowed him to avoid being shocked, he took advantage of the situation. However, keep in mind that he never learned under these circumstances whether or not the situation was in reality still dangerous. Again, avoidance behavior is self-reinforcing because it reduces anxiety.

One is reminded of the delusional individual who was standing on a street corner snapping his fingers over and over again. A policeman approached him and asked, "What are you doing?"

The disturbed person answered, "Keeping the elephants away."

"By snapping your fingers?"

"Yes."

"There's no elephants around here."

"Right. Works good, doesn't it?"

The only way you will learn that a fear is groundless or that a worry is useless is to take a bit of a chance and find out if there really is any danger. If your common sense tells you that your fears are foolish, then stand your ground and tolerate as much anxiety as you can, before you quit the psychological field. By doing this, you will gradually build up more and more anxiety tolerance.

ACTING AND BRAVERY

Act More Bravely Than You Feel. In the musical play *The King and I,* Anna's young son is afraid to enter the kingdom of Siam. He has heard that the population consists largely of barbarians. Anna tells him, in song, that when she is afraid, "I whistle a happy tune." The song points out that if we make believe we're brave, then we may be as brave as we make believe we are.

Anna's advice sounds a little illogical at first. Common sense tells us that we feel and then behave, not the other way around. The standard example is we see a bear in the forest, feel afraid, and run. However, William James, a principal founder of American psychology, said that the opposite is also true. The act of running away from the bear makes us feel afraid. This is known as the *James-Lange theory*, named after both William James and the Danish physiologist Carl Lange. Running increases nervous system arousal, increases the pumping action of the heart, and in our excitement we feel fear more intensely.

It is said, "The coward dies a thousand deaths, the brave person only one." And we all know that in a crowded theater when there is a fire alarm it is better to walk than to run. Running induces panic, an intense emotional reaction.

When you are in any situation that induces anxiety such as a job interview or a difficult examination, will your body to go through the external motions of a person who is calm and in control. You will find that the overt actions feed back upon your emotional state and you will feel less apprehensive.

Putting the confidence cart before the worry horse often makes a bit of psychological sense.

SLOWING DOWN

When You Feel Like Hurrying Up, Slow Down. You are under time pressure. You are dressing for an important appointment. You have to turn a project in by 4 o'clock. You are driving on the freeway and you are late for work. You are worried that you will not meet the timetable. It is a natural reaction to hurry up. Actually, this is a good way to increase your sense of nervous frazzle. It is *not* a good way to calm down and get things done. When you hurry up you automatically make yourself more excited. And you are more likely to make mistakes, get in an accident, or botch up your work.

Hurrying up when you are under time pressure is the natural, unreflected response. Slowing down when you feel like hurrying up is paradoxical. But if you try it you will experience an almost instant balm on your nervous irritation.

OTHER ROLE MODELS

Practice Voluntary Disidentification, Then Consciously Identify With Models Other Than the Ones in Your Life Who Worry to Excess. If you have been identifying with a parent or a sibling who worries too much, decide that you are going to voluntarily disidentify from that person. Sally C. had the mother who worried about gaining weight and growing old. Sally has adopted some of the same worries. Sally can say to herself, "Mom is Mom and I am me. We're two different persons. Her feelings are her own feelings. And mine are my own. She doesn't experience my life and I don't experience hers. We're two different individuals." She can put these ideas in writing from time to time, and this will facilitate the disidentification process.

Now Sally needs to pick one or several role models she can admire and desire to imitate to some extent. These role models can come from people Sally knows, from movies, from novels, and from biographies. The role models should be persons who, at least to all appearances, have poise, self-confidence, and who worry very little.

BEHAVIORAL REHEARSAL

Practice Before You Perform. This is known as *behavioral rehearsal*. Before actors put on a play for the general public they rehearse several times and even usually have a dress rehearsal. They still have opening night jitters and often some stage fright. But imagine how much they would worry before the performance if they had not rehearsed.

Let's say that you are to give a talk in a public-speaking class tomorrow. Give the talk to an emotionally supportive friend. Let's say that you are going to take a difficult test in a few days. Write out questions and answers and rehearse the answers. Let's say that you will be interviewed for a job soon. Write out a script trying to imagine what you will be asked and how you will respond. Make two copies and act out the interview, again with an emotionally supportive friend.

You will worry less about the situation you are facing, and you will be more confident in the situation.

The Last Word

The general theme of this chapter has been that chronic worry is a habit, a maladaptive one. The Swiss philosopher and poet Henri Frédéric Amiel wrote, "To learn new habits is everything, for it is to reach the substance of life. Life is but a tissue of habits."

You *can* learn new habit patterns, patterns that will undermine irrational fear and excessive worry.

Key Points to Remember

□— The tendency toward compulsive worry is a *habit*, a cluster of related learned responses.

□— Some fears may be understood in terms of the process of *classical conditioning*, a process involving the association of stimuli. A fear acquired in this way may be identified as a conditioned emotional reaction.

□— A partial explanation of a neurotic process is to understand it in terms of conditioned avoidance behavior.

□— The tendency to worry excessively is often in part due to *observational learning*, a process in which we assimilate behavior patterns by watching others and taking many of our cues from them.

□— Practice voluntary systematic desensitization.

□— Voluntarily work on disconnecting adversely associated ideas.

□— Use counterconditioning.

□— Practice voluntary nonavoidance.

□— Act more bravely than you feel.

□— When you feel like hurrying up, slow down.

□— Practice voluntary disidentification. Then consciously identify with models other than the ones in your life who worry to excess.

□— Practice before you perform.

5 INDUCING RELAXATION: LOW AROUSAL CAN'T COEXIST WITH WORRY

I asked a group of introductory psychology students to use the word *relax* in a sentence, and to turn in their written responses. Here are several answers, selected more or less at random, from those I received out of a group of thirty-five:

1. I can't relax no matter how hard I try.

2. Relax! Relax! The doctors say, "Relax." The therapists say, "Relax." But they don't tell you how.

3. I've always been a calm, relaxed person. And I can't understand why other people are so uptight.

4. My husband is nice and relaxed. But then I do all of the worrying for him.

5. The world is a little crazy, a kind of madhouse. How can you relax in a madhouse?

6. It makes me tense to think about relaxing.

7. When I want to relax I go to the seashore and spend some time looking at the waves.

As you can see from the above sentences, the concept of relaxation elicits quite a spectrum of outlooks and ideas.

Some people have a kind of natural calm, a placid disposition. Some have discovered effective ways to induce relaxation. However, others find it difficult to relax. It is very common to have this problem. It is one of the reasons that *antianxiety drugs*, also known as the *minor tranquilizers*, are so popular. More than sixty million prescriptions a year are written for these agents. One of the principal effects of many of these drugs is that they induce muscle relaxation. And it has been found in clinical work that muscle relaxation is antagonistic to anxiety.

Another effect of these drugs is that they lower central nervous system arousal. You are likely to be less vigilant, your pulse slows down, and your respiration slows down. This is experienced psychologically as "calm" in contrast to "excitement." When you perceive yourself as calm, you are, by definition, not worrying.

Although relaxation can be induced with prescription drugs, it can also be induced through self-directed psychological techniques. These techniques consist of a set of learnable skills. If you can acquire these skills, you have learned the art of relaxation. Drugs may in some cases have adverse side effects. Consequently, there often is an advantage to finding drug-free ways to relax.

Also, learning the art of relaxation gives you a sense of self-mastery. It does good things for your self-esteem.

The Autonomic Nervous System

It will help you to acquire relaxation skills if you have an understanding of how the autonomic nervous system works. When applying the methods to be described later, they will make more sense if seen in the light of physiological knowledge.

The *autonomic nervous system* is the division of the nervous system that controls involuntary activities of the body, activities that take place without the use of the will. Examples include the beating of your heart, the digestion of your food, your respiration, and so forth. You don't

give any conscious attention to these complex biological events, but they take place anyway.

The autonomic nervous system is itself divided into two parts, the *sympathetic* and the *parasympathetic*. As a convenient way to think of their action, imagine that the sympathetic division is the "go" system, and the parasympathetic is the "slow down" system.

Let's say any one of the following things happens. You win some money unexpectedly. A good old friend calls you on the phone. An attractive member of the opposite sex flirts with you. Life presents you suddenly with a difficult problem. You get frustrated and feel angry. In any of these cases, you will probably respond with greater arousal. Psychologically, you will feel somewhat excited. You have hit the gas pedal of the "go" system.

On the other hand, let's say that any of a different set of things happens. You have just eaten a big turkey dinner with all of the trimmings. You are listening to a boring friend describe at length a movie that does not interest you. You have had an extra glass of wine with a meal. You are watching a rerun of a situation comedy that you never much liked in the first place. In any of these cases, you will probably respond with reduced arousal.

Psychologically, you will fell bored and calm. You have hit the brakes of the "slow down" system.

The sympathetic and the parasympathetic divisions of the autonomic nervous system have antagonistic actions. They are like a seesaw. When one side is up the other is down. You can decrease sympathetic activity by inducing greater activity in the parasympathetic division.

Although you do not have direct voluntary control over the activity of the autonomic nervous system, you do have indirect voluntary control. For example, if you say to your heart, "Beat more rapidly, beat more rapidly, beat more rapidly," it will not respond to these instructions. But if you will yourself to walk at a rapid rate or to run for a while, you will find that your pulse rate has increased. By an act of will you have caused your heart to respond. But you had to take an *indirect* nervous system route. The increased heart rate is sympathetic activity.

By the same logic, it is possible to take an indirect route and activate the parasympathetic division. This will lead to lower arousal. And as already noted, lower arousal is incompatible with anxiety and worry.

The self-directed methods to be described in this chapter are all designed to activate the parasympathetic division of the autonomic nervous system.

Meditation and Self-Hypnosis

For many centuries, yogis in India and Zen masters in Japan have used meditation as a way of inducing an altered state of consciousness. In these ancient Eastern disciplines, the aim of meditation is primarily to enter into a new relationship with either the universe or oneself. In yoga, the aim is to unite completely with the All. In Zen, the aim is to achieve full understanding and to see beyond the veil of illusion that covers reality. These are ambitious goals, far beyond the scope of this book. However, the meditative tradition has yielded certain skills that can be readily applied in everyday life. Consequently, without regard to any religious tradition or philosophy of life, these meditative skills will be incorporated into the methods to be presented.

Hypnosis started off with bad press because it was associated with the healing activities of an eighteenth-century French charlatan named Franz Anton Mesmer. For many years the word *mesmerize* was a synonym for "hypnotize." Benjamin Franklin and others judged Mesmer's "cures" to be due to the overactive imaginations of his subjects.

The truth is that hypnosis is respected in medical, psychiatric, and clinical psychological practice. It is simply a method of making a subject more amenable to positive suggestions, suggestions that will have a beneficial effect on the individual's life. Almost forty years ago, the Council on Mental Health of the American Medical Association made a favorable report on hypnosis.

The goal of this chapter is not to make you a master hypnotist or a hypnotherapist. However, adapting much of what has been learned about hypnosis, it is possible to induce rather readily a light trance in yourself. In a state of light trance you are completely conscious and in control. The only suggestions employed are those that you have already decided ahead of time to give yourself. These are called *autosuggestions*. Both meditative techniques and self-hypnotic ones are combined in a practical way in the next section. The aim of the techniques is to make you more receptive to your own autosuggestions.

Methods

The principal methods to be described all require certain preconditions.

I. You need a chair, preferably a comfortable one that will allow you to rest your head. However, if no comfortable chair is available, you may use almost any chair. It is not necessary to recline.

However, if you want to use a sofa or a bed instead of a chair, that is acceptable. Experiment and find out what works best for you.

2. You need a quiet place where you are not likely to be disturbed by your partner or children. Take the phone off the hook or let your answering machine take calls. Eliminate external sources of energy such as the television set, bright sunlight streaming in through a window, and so forth. Overall, do your best to lower the general level of environmental stimulation.

3. You need a time out from your regular duties or responsibilities. About ten to fifteen minutes will be required for most of the methods. However, if as little as five minutes is available, a beneficial effect can be obtained with the third method to be described, the *relaxation response*.

PROGRESSIVE RELAXATION

Use Progressive Relaxation. Progressive relaxation is a method that was introduced by Edmund Jacobson, an author and researcher, almost sixty years ago. The method is often called *Jacobson's progressive relaxation*. It has stood the test of time and is often used by psychotherapists to induce deep muscle relaxation. In particular, it is often used as an adjunct to systematic desensitization (see chapter 4). It is a valuable tool for persons who suffer from chronic muscle tension.

Assuming you have met all of the preconditions listed earlier, make yourself comfortable and follow these instructions:

1. Close your eyes.

2. Make your right hand into a fist. Squeeze it more and more tightly as you count slowly to seven.

Now let go and allow your hand to relax to the count of seven, being fully aware of the pleasant relaxed sensation through it. Note that had the instruction been given, "Relax your hand," you would not have been able to do so. This is because you cannot voluntarily relax a muscle that is already at rest. However, you *can* voluntarily tighten or tense a muscle. And then you *can* voluntarily let go of that tension. What Jacobson discovered is that the relaxation of a muscle or muscle group following voluntary contraction is greater than the relaxation associated with the muscle in a prior state of rest. Or, to put it another way, alternating voluntary muscle contraction with a voluntary release induces deep muscle relaxation.

3. Make your whole right arm tense and rigid. Increase the contraction as you count slowly to seven. Now let go and allow your arm to relax to the count of seven, being fully aware of the pleasant relaxed sensation spreading through it.

4. Tighten the muscles around your shoulders and neck. Increase the tension as you count slowly to seven. Now let go and allow your shoulder and neck muscles to relax to the count of seven, being fully aware of the pleasant relaxed sensation spreading through them.

5. Tighten your buttocks, allowing the tightening to include your lower back, if possible. Increase the tension as you count slowly to seven. Now let go and allow these muscles to relax to the count of seven, being fully aware of the pleasant relaxed sensation spreading through them.

6. Tighten the muscles surrounding your belly button and lower abdomen. Increase the tension as you count slowly to seven. Now let go and allow

these muscles to relax to the count of seven, being fully aware of the pleasant relaxed sensation spreading through them.

7. Tightly curl your right toes. Increase the tension as you count slowly to seven. Now let go and allow these muscles to relax to the count of seven, being fully aware of the pleasant relaxed sensation spreading through your foot.

8. Tighten your entire right leg. Increase the tension as you count slowly to seven. Now let go and allow your leg muscles to relax to the count of seven, being fully aware of the pleasant relaxed sensation spreading through your leg.

9. Tightly curl your left toes. Increase the tension as you count slowly to seven. Now let go and allow these muscles to relax to the count of seven, being fully aware of the pleasant relaxed sensation spreading through your foot.

10. Tighten your entire left leg. Increase the tension as you count slowly to seven. Now let go and allow your leg muscles to relax to the count of seven, being fully aware of the pleasant relaxed sensation spreading through your leg.

11. You have now completed the progressive relaxation of the key muscle groups. Now just enjoy the pleasant state of relaxation that has been spreading through your whole body. Stay in this state for at least several minutes. When you are ready to come out of the state, slowly stretch your arms and legs. Rotate your head slowly and languidly. Enjoy the stretching sensations as you allow your body to return to a state of everyday readiness. Open your eyes, stand slowly, and, taking some time to pace yourself, resume your normal activities.

AUTOGENIC TRAINING

Use Autogenic Training. Autogenic training is a self-hypnotic procedure characterized by mental autosuggestions.

The method was developed in the 1930s in Germany by Dr. Johannes H. Schultz as a systematic way to help people relax. It has been found to be a useful adjunct method in the treatment of various disorders including digestive problems, alcohol abuse, sleep problems, and fatigue. It is designed to refresh the individual. Autogenic training periods should last about ten minutes, and, ideally, the method should be used twice a day.

Assuming you have met all of the preconditions listed earlier directly below the heading "Methods," make yourself comfortable and follow these instructions:

1. Close your eyes.

2. Say to yourself, "I am at peace." Repeat this three or four times.

3. Pick the hand and arm that are normally dominant in your behavior. In other words, if you are right-handed, pick this hand and arm. Now concentrate on your hand and say to yourself, "My hand is heavy and warm." Repeat this autosuggestion three times. Now concentrate on your arm and say to yourself, "My arm is heavy and warm." Evidence from research on biofeedback training indicates that such autosuggestions actually have the effect of inducing blood vessels to dilate. This expansion is associated with increased blood flow. Increased blood flow is in turn associated with muscle relaxation.

4. Now concentrate on your left hand and say to yourself, "My left hand is heavy and warm." Repeat this autosuggestion three times. Continue in the same manner, concentrating on the left

arm, the right foot, the right leg, the left foot, and the left leg.

5. When you have made the circuit of all of the extremities say to yourself, "The heaviness and warmth are spreading gently toward my neck, back, and abdominal muscles." Repeat this auto-suggestion three times.

6. Say to yourself, "I am at peace. I am enjoying the gentle pleasure of the heaviness and the warmth." Repeat this autosuggestion three times. Say to yourself, "My pulse is calm and strong." Repeat this autosuggestion three times.

7. Now say to yourself, "My body and my mind are drifting in a cloudless mental sky." Repeat this autosuggestion three times. Enjoy the sensation of being detached and relaxed. Stay in this state for at least several minutes.

8. When you are ready to come out of the state, say to yourself, "The heaviness and the warmth are fading away from my hands, feet, arms, and legs. The heaviness and warmth are fading away from my body. I am ready to return to normal activity." Repeat this autosuggestion three times. Stretch your arms and legs slowly. Take a deep breath and exhale. In autogenic training, Step 8 is called the *return*, and should be executed slowly.

Note: If, when making autosuggestions, you find your-self thinking of other things or losing the focus of your attention, don't get angry at yourself. This is natural. Just bring your attention back to the autosuggestions and continue.

THE RELAXATION RESPONSE

Induce the Relaxation Response. The relaxation response was studied extensively about twenty years ago by Herbert

Benson of the Harvard Medical school. He was doing research on a form of Eastern meditation known as *transcendental meditation* or TM. He found that transcendental meditation tends to elicit an innate pattern that Benson called the *relaxation response*. It is a response that neutralizes the effects of the *fight-or-flight* reaction, itself a natural reaction to a threat. It is this latter reaction that is associated with anxiety and worry. It is valuable when a threat is objective. However, it is also called into play by irrational fears and useless worries. In brief, the fight-or-flight reaction increases activity in the sympathetic division of the autonomic nervous system, making the individual excited. The relaxation response, on the other hand, activates the parasympathetic division of the autonomic nervous system, making the individual calm.

Benson found that it is not necessary to use transcendental meditation to induce the relaxation response. It can be done without reference to any particular esoteric tradition.

In order to induce the relaxation response, be sure that you have met all of the preconditions listed earlier directly below the heading "Methods," make yourself comfortable, and follow these instructions:

1. Close your eyes.

2. Become aware of your breathing. Do not change its rate, just be aware.

3. Select a focus word in order to help you concentrate your attention. I suggest that the selected word be *relax* for several reasons: (1) This is your aim, relaxation, (2) the word has two syllables, making it convenient to use in connection with our two-stage breathing cycle, and (3) repetition of the word itself acts as an autosuggestion.

4. As you inhale, think "Re-," the first half of *relax*.

5. As you exhale, think "-lax," the second half of *relax*.

6. Continue in this manner for about three to seven minutes. As indicated, a beneficial effect can be obtained if even as little as three minutes is available. It's all right to sneak a peek at your watch or a convenient clock in order to monitor your time. This won't be enough to make you come out of your relaxed state.

7. When you are ready to come out of the state, keep your eyes closed for a little while. Just let your mind drift and allow it to wander as you get ready to open your eyes. Stretch and take a few deep breaths. Before you open your eyes, say to yourself, "I'm feeling relaxed. When I open my eyes I will feel alert and ready to function."

Induction of the relaxation response is extremely easy using the above approach. One of its principal advantages is that it can be used by busy people in almost any situation.

Although the induction method described has no autosuggestions directed toward the muscles, it does nonetheless tend to relax them. By lowering central nervous system arousal, there is a spreading effect outward. And the muscles tend to relax automatically.

Common-Sense Methods

It is, of course, possible to induce muscle relaxation without the use of a hypnotic approach. Two common-sense methods are identified below.

MODERATE EXERCISE

Engage in Moderate Exercise. An example of moderate exercise is taking a brisk 15- to 20-minute walk. Brisk walking is aerobic, and it also automatically puts muscles on alert as they come into play. After you finish exercising, sit in a comfortable chair, close your eyes, and allow

yourself to daydream without any attempt to control the course of mental events. Your body will automatically relax. Walking has increased the activity of the sympathetic division of the autonomic nervous system. Sitting with your eyes closed automatically switches on the antagonistic action of the parasympathetic division of the autonomic nervous system. Relaxation follows without conscious effort.

Also, note that moderate exercise fosters the formation of *endorphins*, chemical messengers in the brain that give you a sense of well-being.

A WARM BATH

Take a Warm Bath. If you take a warm bath, your muscles will automatically relax. Warmth dilates blood vessels, resulting in greater blood flow to limbs and extremities.

A variant on taking a warm bath is to soak in a spa or hot tub. There are potential problems that should be noted. First, some people set the temperature too high and soak too long. This will make you so relaxed that you'll try to return to normal functioning with all of the get up and go of a wet noodle. Don't overdo it.

Second, some people have a drink or two while in a hot tub. This can be a dangerous practice, particularly when alone. Soaking in the tub lowers arousal. Drinking alcohol lowers arousal. The two factors interact and have a multiplicative effect on each other, and it is possible to grow faint and lose consciousness. Alone, it is even possible to slip down into the tub and drown. A certain amount of common sense and natural caution is called for.

The Last Word

The first time that you attempt to induce relaxation by one of the methods described in this chapter, you may obtain mixed results. Some relaxation will probably occur, but you may be somewhat less than satisfied. Research on hypnotic techniques suggests that they are a kind of conditioning, and conditioning requires learning.

If you were taking piano lessons, you would not expect to play fluently the first time that you ran through an assigned piece of music. But, with repetition and practice, you would become fluent and confident. So it is with the relaxation methods described. Each time you use one of them, you will find that you obtain a more rapid, and more complete, beneficial effect.

Key Points to Remember

□— Although relaxation can be induced with prescription drugs, it can also be induced through self-directed psychological techniques.

□— The *autonomic nervous system* is the division of the nervous system that controls involuntary activities of body. The system is divided into two parts. The *sympathetic* subdivision is the "go" system. The *parasympathetic* subdivision is the "slow down" system.

□— The meditative tradition has yielded certain skills that can be applied in everyday life.

□— Self-hypnotic techniques are a useful way of giving yourself positive autosuggestions.

□— Use progressive relaxation.

□— Use autogenic training.

□— Induce the relaxation response.

□— Two common-sense ways to relax are: (1) engage in moderate exercise and (2) take a warm bath.

6 OUR MENTAL LIVES: "I THINK, THEREFORE I WORRY"

Imagine a huge shark swimming in its natural habitat. Is it worried? Of course not. It is lord of all that it surveys and the master of its environment. If it sees into the future at all, which seems unlikely, it sees only a short distance—and dimly. Even if a hunting trip is being planned against it by human beings, it is not worried. It knows nothing about human ways and has no warning system for such possibilities. As far as we know, a shark is incapable of analytical thought.

Now think about yourself in your natural habitat. Are you king or queen of all that you survey and the master of your environment? The answer is self-evident. Can you see into the future, or imagine that you can? Yes, that's one of the drawbacks of being able to think. You think about what *might* happen. But it's also one of the advantages of being able to think. Thinking about what might happen makes you vigilant and allows you to prepare ahead of time for potential threats to your well being. And our tendency to worry has its roots in this valuable ability.

The seventeenth-century philosopher René Descartes wrote, "I think, therefore I am." He could have added, "I think, therefore I worry." It would seem that we're in some kind of a trap. Thinking being a natural tendency of the human mind, it appears that we can't escape worry. Well, of course we can't escape the kind of worry that is based on realistic fears. We don't *want* to escape that kind of worry, because it is functional.

However, the kind of chronic worry that is the subject of this book is *not* based on realistic fears. Excessive worry is useless and arises to a large extent from *cognitive errors*, well-known tendencies in our mental life to distort reality and cause us emotional difficulties. It is this kind of thinking, the kind associated with cognitive errors, that will be examined in this chapter. And you will discover practical ways to cope with these errors.

If thinking causes many of your useless worries, than thinking itself can be used to modify or eliminate these worries. You can learn to fight psychological fire with psychological fire.

Self-Directed Mental Strategies

In the pages that follow you will find a group of self-directed mental strategies that will help you counter the worst effects of cognitive distortions. At this point, it will be helpful to make a distinction between reactive thinking and constructive thinking.

Reactive thinking is thinking without analysis. It is just running off what the psychiatrist Aaron Beck, an eminent cognitive therapist, calls *automatic thoughts*. An automatic thought may be looked upon as a "mental conditioned reflex." A stimulus is experienced, and the thought flows forth involuntarily. This is an example from Beck's work: A man with an irrational fear of dogs sees one and thinks, "It's going to bite me." He feels fear; his heart begins to pound and he wants to run. The thought induces the fear. The odd thing is that the dog is only a poodle and it is *locked behind a chain-link fence*. The man will be a victim of fear as long as he allows his thought to flow in a reactive manner.

Constructive thinking has several valuable attributes. It is reality-oriented. It is logical. And it is productive.

However, it does require *voluntary* mental action. There is nothing automatic about it. You have to *decide* to think in a constructive manner. The man who sees the dog behind the chain-link fence must voluntarily replace the fear-arousing automatic thought with the constructive thought, "It can't bite me if it's locked behind a fence." When this new thought is substituted for the old one, fear will subside.

THOUGHTS ABOUT THE EXTERNAL WORLD

Remember That Your Thoughts About the External World Are Not the World Itself. External world? What other kind of world is there? Why not just say "world?" There *is* another world—it is the *psychological world*, the inner world created by your thoughts and your perceptions. Alfred Korzybski, founder of a systematic way of coping with thought and life called *general semantics*, was fond of saying, "The map is not the territory." What he meant by this is that your psychological world is like a map. The external world is like a territory that relates to a map. But it is of great importance to realize that the map and the territory, the psychological world and the external world, are *not identical*. If you clearly understand and recognize this, you will be set free to some extent from adverse emotional reactions, including excessive worry. You will see that *the way you think* has a lot to do with the way you feel. And you will see that if your "map" is incorrect or distorted, you will have problems. You will also understand that it is within your power to rewrite and redraw the map in such a way that it fits better with the territory ("reality," or the external world).

Remembering that your thoughts about the external world are not the world itself is itself a mental strategy. And it provides a solid foundation for the balance of the self-directed mental strategies to follow.

CATASTROPHIC THINKING

Avoid Catastrophic Thinking. Catastrophic thinking, identified in particular by the New York psychotherapist Albert Ellis, is characterized by thoughts and images that point toward the worst happening. Robin C. is driving and hears an odd, unfamiliar sound from the motor. She begins to think, "That's an odd sound. I wonder what it means. Maybe the motor is going to catch on fire. Maybe I'll get stranded by the side of the road or, worse, trapped in a burning car."

The individual who is prone to catastrophic thinking is like Chicken Little in the fable for children. An acorn falls on Chicken Little's head, and soon he is proclaiming to the whole barnyard, "The sky is falling! The sky is falling!" The other chickens, being suggestible, begin to repeat, "The sky is falling! The sky is falling!" Soon all the chickens are in a state of mass hysteria.

Catastrophic thinking is due to a common tendency to *overgeneralize.* One case or instance is taken as the sign predicting a whole group of similar cases or instances. A well-known proverb can be mentally recited as one strategy to counter overgeneralization. The proverb is, "One swallow doesn't make a summer." The appearance of a single indicator should not be seen as providing enough information to reach a conclusion.

MURPHY'S LAW

Reject Murphy's Law. Murphy's Law, a kind of negative joke and part of the national folklore, says, "If anything can go wrong, it will." We hear this statement, think it's clever, see some truth in it, and laugh. The problem is that it can get to be a way of thinking. I have known people who are fond of citing Murphy's Law. They're always looking for the worst in everything and tend to have a pessimistic outlook. Murphy's Law is itself simply a different version of catastrophic thinking. Unexamined, Murphy's Law can have a corrosive effect on your life.

The way to reject Murphy's Law is to say to yourself, "I'm writing a new law, the Anti-Murphy Law. This new law says, "If anything can go right, it will." You may say that this new law is unrealistic and overly optimistic. But think about it. *Usually* things do go right. Most people who leave for work get there. Most babies are born without birth defects. Most of the time when you eat you don't get a gastrointestinal infection. So the Anti-Murphy Law is, in general, more realistic than Murphy's Law. Consciously reciting the Anti-Murphy Law will help you to bring down your worry temperature.

EITHER-OR THINKING

Refrain from Either-Or Thinking. Either-or thinking is also known as "black-white thinking" and "yes-no" thinking. It is essentially thinking in two and only two categories. It is an error because only a little reflection reveals that many of life's situations and outcomes can more properly be evaluated in terms of a gradient, a scale with several measurements. In the visual world, black and white are not the only two measures of brightness. We all recognize that we can go from black to dark gray to medium gray to light gray to white. And there are even shades of gray in between.

So it is in the psychological world. Situations and outcomes ought to be evaluated in shades of gray. Rochelle D., a first-grade teacher, has been asked to give a talk on current trends in grammar school education to a service club. She has a B.A. in psychology and a state teaching credential. She is highly qualified to give the talk. Nonetheless, she finds herself ruminating the night before the scheduled presentation: "I know I'm going to make a fool of myself. If they laugh at me, I don't know what I'll do. I'll just die, I guess. I won't be able to stand it. I'll fall through the floor. I know my mind is going to go blank." Rochelle seems to be thinking that either her talk will be a big hit or it will be a complete failure. She needs to recognize that it is just a modest little talk, one of many that the club hears during the course of a year. And it will probably be received with at least polite interest.

PERFECTIONISM

Reject the Doctrine of Perfectionism. The doctrine of perfectionism states that our actions and accomplishments must always reach the 100 percent mark. If you accept perfectionism, you must *always* do the right thing as a parent, *never* make a bad decision, earn straight A's in school, and so forth. Perfectionistic thinking can cause great anxiety.

Tamara N. wrote poetry. She had accumulated over a period of a year about fifty very special poems that she wrote, rewrote, and rewrote again. She kept trying to make them a little better, and then a little better, and then a little better—in short, perfect. Her sister kept encouraging Tamara to send the poems in to a particular magazine.

Tamara kept thinking, "They're not good enough. They need more work."

Then Tamara typed one of the poems, determined to send it in. (She didn't own a word processor.) She typed the poem fifteen times because of minor corrections she had to make and because she wasn't happy with the centering. She was thinking, "It's not neat enough. It doesn't look right on the page." At long last the poem was sent in and quickly accepted by an admiring editor who was lavish in her praise.

BEING WELL-LIKED

Accept the Idea That You Will Be Well-Liked by Some People and Disliked by Others. On the job, in the family, and among friends and acquaintances, the person prone to chronic worry often tends to worry about being well-liked. Ursula T. has just received a put-down from a coworker named Ruby. Ursula's automatic thought is, "Ruby doesn't like me. I can't *stand* it. I don't know how I can go on working with her. My day is ruined. I've got to get back in her good graces." Then Ursula begins to worry about *how* to get back in Ruby's good graces. The truth in all of this is that Ursula is being rather silly. She is making herself into a patsy. She needs to think something such as, "So what if Ruby doesn't like me. That's her problem. And just because she made the mistake of putting me down doesn't mean that she doesn't like me. Maybe she was in a grouchy mood and I was just in the way. But even if she doesn't like me, so what? I can certainly stand to not be liked by a few people."

EXTERNAL FACTORS

Avoid the Idea That Your Anxiety and Worry Are Caused by External Factors. Anxiety and worry seem to have their sources in the external world. You think, "Well, of course *anyone* would be worried in *this* situation." But it's not true. Situations that make you tense or hyperconcerned may very well be faced with equanimity and calm by others. It *seems* that it's the external world that causes your feeling state, but it's your *evaluation* of external factors that is the real cause. Rochelle, asked to give a talk, experiences apprehension. And she thinks that this is because she was asked to give a talk. But that's not so. It is her *beliefs* about the talk that cause her apprehension. It is what she says to herself in her own mind that makes her heart pound. Another person, an experienced public speaker, would feel no apprehension in the same situation as Rochelle.

Emery F. wants to ask Marcella, a coworker, out on a date. He thinks, "She probably won't want to go out with me. She'll probably turn me down. And then I'll be the laughingstock of the office." These thoughts induce anxiety as he debates with himself the pros and cons of actually revealing his feelings to Marcella. Derek S. wants to ask Lora, a coworker, to go out on a date. He thinks, "I think she likes me. I can tell she's been flirting with me. And if I'm wrong, and she turns me down, so what? Nothing ventured, nothing gained." Derek will be prompt to act and feel no apprehension. The objective situation is the same for both men. Yet one man is filled with apprehension, and the other is confident. What is the difference? Again, the difference resides in their beliefs about the situation.

PERSONAL CONSTRUCTS

Rewrite Personal Constructs. The importance of personal constructs in personality was emphasized by the psychologist George Kelly. A *personal construct* is a group of related ideas that one has about oneself, and it has much to with how you perceive, believe, and act as you adjust to the various challenges of life. We have a set of personal constructs, and they are key elements in the makeup of our personalities. A given construct can be negative or positive. If a construct is negative, it is identical to what Alfred Adler, a pioneer in psychotherapy, called an *inferiority complex*. Examples of negative personal constructs are: "I'm no good at math," "I'm not pretty," "I'm a slow learner," "I'm short," "I'm not clever," "I have no talent," and so forth. As you venture forth to cope with life, the presence of one or several negative personal constructs can only cause you anxiety and aggravate your worry tendencies.

Examples of positive personal constructs are: "I'm a competent person," "I'm well liked and have a pleasing personality," "I'm as bright as the next person," "I have enough of what it takes to reach my goals," and so forth.

A common negative personal construct is, "I'm inadequate to the task. I don't have the talent, or the ability, or the knowledge to complete this job." Let's call this the *incompetency construct*. If you are a parent, the incompetency construct will cause you to be uncertain and apprehensive as you raise your children. If you are a student, the incompetency construct undermines any joy you might obtain from the learning process.

In order to rewrite the incompetency construct, think of the famous story for children called *The Little Engine That Could*. As the little engine is called in to substitute for a big, powerful engine that has broken down, it is filled with doubt. It doesn't know if it can pull the long trainload of toys up the mountain that must be climbed and then descended to reach children waiting for the toys. As it chugs up the mountain it is filled with doubt. It suffers from the incompetency construct. *It doesn't think it is adequate to the task*. But then it focuses on the goal, delivering the toys to the waiting children. It is filled with desire to fulfill its wonderful mission. Doubt begins to turn into confidence. It starts to say to itself, over and over again, "I think I can. I think I can. I think I can." And it finds that *it can!* It reaches the crest of the mountain with great effort, but *it reaches it*. As it descends happily into the valley it basks in its success by saying, "I thought I could. I thought I could. I thought I could." Although this is a story written for children, think of it also as a story written for the child that still resides within you. You can use the story's inspirational message to help you rewrite personal constructs from negative ones into positive ones.

The important thing to realize about personal constructs is that although they *feel* like reality, they are not reality itself. They are your "personal constructions" *about* reality. You made them up. They did, of course, come from somewhere. Negative personal constructs came from bad experiences. But it is quite possible that you reached the wrong conclusions, that you overgeneralized, and your self-image is unnecessarily worse than it ought to be.

You can consciously rewrite your personal constructs. You can target a negative one and ask yourself, "Is it really true? What are the facts? Can I rewrite this construct and convert it into a positive one? You might be surprised to find out that the answers to these questions will allow you to get over some of your doubts and insecurities that feed worry behavior.

MAGNIFICATION

Stop Magnifying the Size of Your Worries. Magnification is a cognitive distortion in which every problem seems bigger than it really is. Risks seem greater than they really are. Magnification tends to inflate what ought to be a realistic concern into a full-blown, oversized worry. We have all heard the saying "Stop making mountains out of molehills." If you have a tendency to do this, you have to take the saying seriously and, indeed, *stop* the automatic magnification process.

I am reminded of a cartoon I once saw. It showed an older person standing and looking at two objects. One was an enormous rock. The other was a pebble. The rock had a sign on it that said, "Things I worried about." The pebble's sign said, "Things that actually happened."

DAY-TIGHT COMPARTMENTS

Live in Day-Tight Compartments. Dale Carnegie, author of *How to Win Friends and Influence People*, told the story of a voyage on a great ocean liner. The passengers were taken on a tour of the huge vessel. One of the passengers asked the guide what would happen if the ship hit an iceberg. The answer given was that the ship's hull consisted of a series of watertight compartments. If there was a hole in a section of the hull, it was possible to seal off that section, and the ship would still be able to float. Although anything was possible, this design strategy greatly reduced the risk of sinking. It occurred to Carnegie that the same logic could be applied to worry.

Carnegie recognized that much worry arises from a tendency to think in terms of not only tomorrow, but the day after tomorrow, and even the day after that. Some people are even hyperconcerned about events that are years off. And so, from a psychological point of view, they borrow trouble. They don't live today at all. They neglect the pleasures and satisfactions of the present because they are overly vigilant and preoccupied by the shape of things to come. For persons with these kinds of thought processes, Carnegie recommended the strategy of living in day-tight compartments. Seal off the future as much as possible if you are making yourself sick with worry. Seal it off to keep from sinking. Decide to focus on the present. Let tomorrow take care of itself.

When some people hear about day-tight compartments, they object. "But you *have* to plan for the future. You can't just stop thinking about your goals, paying off your loans, and so forth." Of course. But you don't have to make yourself into a nervous wreck either. And worry is not the same as healthy concern. The very *effort* to think in terms of day-tight compartments will have a beneficial effect if you're a worry-prone person. It will dampen your anxiety.

Once when I was in a business establishment I saw a sign on the wall that said, "Today is the tomorrow we worried about yesterday." The message conveyed by the sign seemed very wise to me, and it captures the essence of living in day-tight compartments.

RECOGNIZING AUTOMATIC THOUGHTS

Train Yourself to Recognize Automatic Thoughts. Unfortunately, worry-causing automatic thoughts are just that, *automatic.* As already noted, they are mental conditioned reflexes. They are like flying fish that pop briefly out of the water and then sink back down below the surface. Automatic thoughts pop out of your subconscious mind, flit through your conscious mind, and then plop down into your subconscious again.

In a flash you think, "Everything's going to go wrong now," or, "I'm going to go broke," or, "They don't like me," or something else that gives you anxious pause.

Imagine that you have a psychological net capable of catching the "flying fish" of the automatic thought. As the thought flashes by, snare it. Now examine it with an objective eye. Is it true? Do you actually think it correctly represents the facts? There will be more about how to challenge automatic thoughts, and the irrational beliefs associated with them, later in this chapter.

DISTANCING

Distance Yourself from Automatic Thoughts. Normally we think of thoughts as our own. Most of us would agree with the sentence "I think my own thoughts." But automatic thoughts do *not* arise from your ego, the "I" of your personality. I say this because you don't *will* them. They are involuntary mental acts, as I said before, mental conditioned reflexes. You need to realize that they are running you. You are not running them. Consequently, in distancing yourself from an automatic thought say to yourself, "I am not willing this thought. It is just happening. I want to alienate myself from it, disown it. It is not me and I am not it. It doesn't represent my real belief. The thought is toxic, causes me to worry unnecessarily, and I reject it."

THE ABC SYSTEM

Use the ABC System of Emotional Self-Management. The ABC system of emotional self-management was devised by Albert Ellis, and it forms an integral part of his approach to psychotherapy, known as *rational-emotive behavior therapy*. The ABC system is of particular value because it is something beneficial that you can do for yourself. It brings together in one unified system the various tips and coping strategies already presented in this chapter.

The A, B, and C in the system are used as keys to help you remember the general outlines of the system.

A stands for *activating event*. An activating event is a fact. It takes place in the external world. It is something that you really see, hear, taste, touch, or smell. Let's go back to Rochelle D., the first-grade teacher who had been asked to give a talk on current trends in grammar school education to a service club. This is the activating event. The fact that she has been asked to give the talk is a fact.

B stands for *belief*. The belief is one that is triggered by A, the activating event. The belief can be rational or irrational. A rational belief is one that is logical, informed, and makes a good fit with actual circumstances. An irrational belief is one that reflects the various cognitive errors discussed earlier. Automatic thoughts tend to be irrational because they do not contain an element of reflection. Rochelle's thoughts are irrational and automatic. You will recall that she thought, "I know I'm going to make a fool of myself. If they laugh at me, I don't know what I'll do. I'll just die, I guess. I won't be able to stand it. I'll fall through the floor. I know my mind is going to go blank."

C stands for *consequence*. The consequence is an *emotional* consequence. In Rochelle's case the consequence is anxiety. The combination of irrational thoughts and anxiety is what we call worry. In most cases this is where the chain of events stops. Worry is a kind of psychological whirlpool. And it just goes around and around with you, its victim, trapped in it. Please note that up until this point the entire sequence A, B, C has been like a domino effect. A causes B to occur. B causes C to occur. And that's it.

Now we need to put in a fourth step. This step is identified as D, and it stands for *dispute*. This fourth step is the step that most victims of chronic worry don't take. As its name suggests, the fourth step requires that you actively dispute the irrational thoughts at point B. This requires an act of will. D requires constructive thought, and constructive thought is antagonistic to the reactive thought that has produced anxiety.

How do you dispute irrational beliefs effectively? Go back and use this chapter as a guide. The various self-directed mental strategies already described are your weapons. With them you can dispute and confront irrational beliefs. You can neutralize their adverse effect on your emotions.

The Last Word

The approach taken in this chapter has a long and solid history behind it. It is inspired and informed by a respected philosophical tradition called *stoicism*. Stoicism asserts that it is not events in themselves that cause misery and unhappiness. It is our evaluation of those events.

Epictetus was a Greek philosopher and a Roman slave. As a slave, he had to learn to cope with adverse circumstances beyond his control, and his observations form important foundation stones for stoicism. Almost 2,000 years ago Epictetus said, "Seek not good from without; seek it within yourselves, or you will never find it." Don't wait for circumstances to change. Don't passively wish for "things to get better." Change the way you think about circumstances. You will worry less and you will feel better about your life.

Key Points to Remember

□—┉ Excessive worry is useless and arises to a large extent from *cognitive errors*, well-known tendencies in our mental life to distort reality and cause emotional difficulties.

▢→ *Reactive thinking* is thinking without analysis. It plays a key role in *automatic thoughts*, thoughts that may be looked upon as "mental conditioned reflexes."

▢→ *Constructive thinking* is reality oriented, logical, and productive. It requires voluntary mental action.

▢→ Remember that your thoughts about the external world are not the world itself.

▢→ Avoid catastrophic thinking.

▢→ Reject Murphy's Law.

▢→ Refrain from either-or thinking.

▢→ Reject the doctrine of perfectionism.

▢→ Accept the idea that you will be well-liked by some people and disliked by others.

▢→ Avoid the idea that your anxiety and worry are caused by external factors.

▢→ Rewrite personal constructs.

▢→ Stop magnifying the size of your worries.

▢→ Live in day-tight compartments.

▢→ Train yourself to recognize automatic thoughts.

▢→ Distance yourself from automatic thoughts.

▢→ Use the ABC system of emotional self-management.

7 EVERYBODY WORRIES: LOOKING AT THE HUMAN PLIGHT WE'RE ALL IN

He was a prince of ancient India approximately 2,500 years ago. His name was Siddhartha Gautama. He reached adolescence, and had never been beyond the palace walls. His father wanted to protect him against the outside world. The youth begged his father to be allowed to make an excursion beyond his secure prison. His father relented, and Siddhartha set forth on horseback with a wise counselor as his guide.

After a time Siddhartha spotted a person, covered with sores, walking along a dirt road. The person was feeble and emaciated. Siddhartha was shocked. He had never seen anything but health and beauty. "What am I seeing?" he asked the counselor.

"You are seeing disease," answered the elder man.

"Could I become diseased?"

"Yes."

A short time later Siddhartha observed a very old person. The individual was wrinkled, bent over, and hobbled along with the aid of a stick. Upset, Siddhartha asked, "What am I seeing?"

"You are seeing old age," answered the companion.

"Might I grow old?"

"Not only might you grow old. You *will* grow old."

Not much time elapsed before the two on horseback passed by a corpse lying by the side of the road. Stunned, Siddhartha asked, "What am I seeing?"

"You are seeing death."

"Is it possible that I too will die?"

"Not only is it possible. You cannot escape death. All who live must die."

Siddhartha had seen enough for the time being, and the two returned to the sanctuary of the castle walls. The king thought that his son would be cured of his affliction, that he would now want to remain where all was safe and predictable.

But Siddhartha was concerned with the human plight we're all in. It appeared that life was suffering, and that there was no escape. Yet he believed that somehow liberation from suffering was possible. He left the castle to become a wanderer and a searcher.

In time, after much experience and meditation, he came to the conclusion that liberation from suffering is to some extent possible if an individual can "blow out" the flame of desire. This state is known as *nirvana*, and the aspirant who has reached this state is free of foolish wants and greed. The individual continues to live, of course, but not in a selfish, avaricious way.

As you probably realized by now, Siddhartha was the original Buddha. *Buddha* means "enlightened one." References to *the* Buddha are to Siddhartha. However, Siddhartha asserted that anyone can be *a* buddha, meaning anyone can achieve a state of enlightenment.

It is certainly not the goal of this chapter to make you into a buddha. Nor is it the goal of this chapter to make a case for the religion known as Buddhism. However, the story of Siddhartha does make several useful points. First, we're all in the same boat. The fact that we all are prone to disease, that we age, and that we inevitably die is a reality that we must cope with in some way. We will either cope poorly, in which case we will suffer more than we need to. Or we will cope effectively, in which case we will not suffer unnecessarily. This chapter is dedicated to the latter approach, and I hope that its down-to-earth suggestions will be genuinely helpful.

   The suggestions owe no allegiance to Eastern philosophy. They are informed to some extent by it, but they are
also largely inspired by a Western philosophical tradition
known as *existentialism*. Existentialism is the point of
view that existence can be understood only in personal,
subjective terms. It is your will and your outlook that
determines whether or not you will suffer more than you
need to, not the way fate cuts the cards and deals them
to you.
   Because the future is by definition uncertain, everybody worries.

I worry.

You worry.

Worry is inescapable. The anxiety surrounding the uncertainty that is part and parcel of life combines with our ability to think in words, and this mixture of emotion and consciousness *is* worry. Nonetheless, having said this, the way in which you approach the realities of the human condition will determine whether or not you worry from time to time in a reality-oriented manner or instead worry on a nagging, chronic basis.

Reducing Existential Anxiety

Existential anxiety is the name given to the kind of anxiety that is woven into the very fabric of life. As its name suggests, it is anxiety associated with existence itself. You can't totally eliminate existential anxiety. But you can reduce it from a consuming fire to a background glow, a level of emotional heat you can at least tolerate. The suggestions that follow are all designed to help you reduce existential anxiety.

ACCEPTING ILLNESS

Accept the Fact That We Are Prone to Illness and Disease. No one wants to be sick. No one wants to contract a chronic illness. Certainly you want to do everything to protect your health and extend your life. Nonetheless, your best efforts may fail. Let's say you are in good health right now. What is your attitude toward the *possibility* of getting sick? Do you think of it as something that *must not* happen? If so, you may be a compulsive worrier about your health. The natural existential anxiety surrounding health combined with the impossible demand that "sickness must not happen to me" combines to create a state known as *hypochondriasis*. Those who suffer from hypochondriasis are miserable. But they are borrowing trouble. They aren't sick, but they are making themselves sick with worry over the possibility that they might get sick.

The proper attitude is to let go of the wish never to be sick. The wish itself is a kind of greed. It is really saying that although other people get sick, you should not. The wish says, "Let it happen to him or her, but not to *me*." It is a kind of selfishness that says, "I am special. I should not be touched by the kinds of woes that other people are touched with." If you are healthy now, enjoy your health while you have it. Odds are you may remain in good health for many, many years. Don't borrow psychological trouble and generate extra anxiety.

What if you have just received a distressing diagnosis? If you are typical, your first response will be *denial*, an ego defense that says, "This isn't true! This *can't* be happening to me. Maybe the lab tests gave a false positive. I want a second opinion." By all means get a second opinion. And it is quite true that the lab tests might have given a false positive. However, if tests and clinical opinion continue to support the first diagnosis, you must at some point accept reality. As long as you are in a state of denial you will intensify existential anxiety. And you will suffer not because you are ill, but because you are suffering emotionally over the fact that you are ill. At some point you must make your peace with the illness, accept it as a fact, and cope with it in a realistic manner. Easier said than done? Of course. However, studies of persons suffering from chronic illnesses suggest that most of them do in fact eventually achieve a level of acceptance and some peace of mind sooner or later. If you recognize the nature of the psychological process, you can reduce existential anxiety sooner rather than later.

ACCEPT AGING

Accept the Fact That We All Age. Anne T., age forty-seven, looks in the mirror and doesn't like what she sees. There are unwanted wrinkles beginning to appear around her eyes and mouth. Her chin is beginning to sag. Gray hairs are starting to appear. A former beauty queen, she thinks, "Can this be me? What's *happening* to me?" What's happening to Anne is that she is aging. It happens to all of us.

The question is, how will Anne cope with aging? Will she try to deny the fact of aging? Will she have a skin peel, a face lift, a tummy tuck, or something else? Will she go to extremes to preserve the illusion of youth? And if she does, who will she be doing it for? Will she be doing if for a husband she fears will be attracted to younger women? Or will she be doing it to fool herself?

The desire to maintain a good appearance is a reasonable one. If Anne dyes her hair, watches her weight, keeps her teeth in good condition, uses a moisturizer on her skin, and so forth, she is being sensible and her behavior is well within normal bounds. On the other hand, if she compulsively searches for the Fountain of Youth with the aid of plastic surgery, she is only aggravating the existential anxiety associated with aging. If the aim of cosmetic surgery is merely to look better, and if this is its only aim, who can argue with it? However, if underlying the surgery is the fantasy that youth is somehow being reclaimed, then this must be recognized as futile. Only a moment's reflection reveals that *plastic surgery adds no years to life.* It does not touch the aging process at all.

Perhaps you saw one of the two movie versions of *Lost Horizon*, based on James Hilton's novel of the same name. The people in Shangri-La, high in the mountains of Tibet, do not age. But if they try to act in a realistic way on their youth by leaving the enchantment of Shangri-La and entering the larger world outside its gates, they age and become old within minutes. Surely one of the messages of *Lost Horizon* is that aging cannot be denied, that hanging on to a youth that is gone is an illusion, and one that can aggravate existential anxiety.

Notice that in the above paragraph I used the phrase *a youth that is gone.* People speak of a "lost" youth. But youth isn't lost. You can't find it after it's gone because it *is* gone. It simply doesn't exist anymore. It is only anxiety-arousing to invest energy in a search for something that doesn't exist.

Carl Jung, one of the early pioneers of psychoanalysis, said that when he was a relatively young man he "felt old age in his bones." Rather than causing him distress, this caused him to feel a sense of joy. He had the intuition that he would live a long life and be able to accomplish his goals and self-assigned tasks. He died in 1961 at the age of eighty-six.

I am reminded of the two friends who had not met in many years. They were now in their eighties. They were both aware of how much they had aged. The first man was a bit of a complainer, a whiner. The second one tended to be an optimist.

The first friend said, "Ah, what a shame. What a sadness. We grew old."

The second friend said, "Oh, stop. Because you didn't die young, you're complaining."

The only way to escape aging is to die young. Aging is the price we pay for living.

ACCEPTING DEATH

Accept the Fact That You Too Will Die. All organisms die. You are an organism. So am I. You will die. So will I. It's just a fact, and if we try to deny it, the denial will only add to our suffering.

I am sure that you have heard of people with who are having their bodies frozen in cryogenic chambers, cotainers capable of maintaining a very low temperature for years.

Aside from serious doubts about whether or not the cryogenic technology will work at all, the whole process is a revelation in how much value many people attach to the survival of their individual egos.

If there is a better life to come after death, then death is not to be feared. The world's great religions teach that we should not want to reside in this mortal coil forever. They indicate that there is a proper time to die.

If, on the other hand, death is oblivion, then death is still not to be feared. Anxiety about death can be reduced by realizing that the oblivion of the ego is a nonexperience. You can experience pain and suffering. But you can't experience oblivion. There is simply no ego to experience it. If this be the nature of death, then death is a nonproblem.

In the movie and play *Death Takes a Holiday*, the character Death, in the form of a human being, says, "And when I call, come bravely through that shadow, and you shall find me only your familiar friend." He says this because he and only he can bring an end to pain and suffering.

Self-destructive behavior, suicidal in nature, that hastens death is certainly pathological. However, it is also self-defeating to deny that death is the natural, inevitable ending to life. The energy that goes into resisting the acceptance of death is wasted. And it is experienced as an intensification of a tendency to worry.

IMPOSSIBLE DEMANDS

Let Go of Impossible Demands. As you can see from what you have already read, it is important to let go of impossible demands. This general theme applies not only to the demand that one not age, be ill, or die. It also applies to many other of life's arenas. Here is a short list of the kinds of impossible demands that some people make in the form of expectations, wishes, and personal dreams:

1. One should have brilliant children who are also attentive and loving.

2. One's partner should always be loving and understanding.

3. One should have an ecstatic sex life.

4. One should have an ideal marriage.

5. One should feel terrific every day.

6. One should never have emotional lows.

7. One should be admired by almost everyone else.

8. One's opinions should always be taken seriously by others.

9. Everything should go right all of the time.

Identified as blatantly as they are in the above list, the sensible reaction is, "But the list is silly." Yes, it is. And that's the point. It *is* silly to make impossible demands on life that cannot be matched by actual events.

And still there is a feeble protest somewhere deep in the human personality. Don't most of us thrill when Don Quixote in the musical play *Man of la Mancha* sings that he dreams the impossible dream, that he yearns to reach the unreachable stars? I remember feeling goose bumps rise when I heard the song performed by Richard Kiley in the title role. Nonetheless, keep in mind that when Don Quixote died he was out of his mind. His totally unrealizable dreams had driven him mad.

Unlike Don Quixote, we should dream the *possible* dream and yearn to reach the *reachable* star. This is the pathway of both a rational life and real hope.

Impossible demands on life are a source of tension and frustration. They increase your level of existential anxiety. If you catch yourself making them, force them to be examined in the glare of reason, and give them up.

FREE WILL

Assert That You Have a Free Will. It is very important for your overall mental health that you assert you have a free will. Free will is both an ancient and a modern doctrine. You will find that St. Thomas Aquinas asserts its importance in his great work the *Summa Theologica* (Theology Summed Up). The French philosopher Jean-Paul Sartre made it a central assumption in his existential philosophy. The psychotherapist Otto Rank, one of Freud's early associates, introduced an approach known as *will therapy* designed to help the individual take direct control of his or her life.

The doctrine of free will is based on the idea that you have the capacity to make real choices in your life. Let's say that Harold, a troubled adolescent, robs a liquor store and threatens the clerk with a gun. There is a ready set of excuses for Harold's behavior. His mother was a prostitute and he never knew his biological father. He did not feel loved and there was no adequate male role model during his developmental years. Or, he has a genetic predisposition that makes him prone to violence. Or, he is short in stature. Consequently, he has an inferiority complex. His peers called him "chicken" and dared him to rob the store. And you can dream up other possible causal factors. It is not that these factors have no significance. But, in the final analysis, did they create a psychological reality so compelling that Harold *had to* hold up the liquor store? The doctrine of free will asserts that they did not, that at all times Harold had a realm of choice, and that he had options well within his own control.

The point of view that opposes the free will doctrine is called determinism. *Determinism* asserts that all behavior is caused. Everything we do can be explained in terms of genetics, blood chemistry, learning experiences, and so forth.

It is certainly not the objective of this section to settle the free will-determinism controversy. However, I do submit that in life as you live it, you do need to take a position. In fact, you *will* take a position, even if it is poorly defined in your own mind. If you act as if you are in charge of your life, you are essentially saying, "I have a free will." If, on the other hand, you act as if you are controlled by external factors, then you are essentially saying, "My behavior is determined."

Research on personality suggests that the deterministic attitude is associated with existential anxiety. Those who adopt it feel that they are helpless pawns of fate, that the winds of destiny blow them hither and yon. They fear for their future and their lives because they feel the way you would feel in a runaway car with no one in the driver's seat.

Similarly, research suggests that the free will attitude is associated with a reduction of existential anxiety. Those who adopt it feel that they are in charge of situations, that they can exercise some degree of control over events.

Don't be concerned about the hard logic of whether or not free will or determinism is "true" in some profound philosophical sense. The psychological reality is that when you act *as if* free will is true, then it is true for you. It becomes a positive, self-fulfilling proposition. And it will help to dispel the miserable cloud of existential anxiety.

TOLERATING AMBIGUITY

Learn to Tolerate Ambiguity. A stimulus is said to be *ambiguous* if it can be perceived in two or more ways. The cards on the Rorschach test are ambiguous stimuli because one person can see a witch on a given card and another person might see a dancing bear on the same card. Life itself is somewhat like a card with an inkblot. It is ambiguous in nature because we live in a world of uncertainty. We can't always be sure that other people like us. We don't know if a business that we have just started with great hope will succeed or fail in the long run. It is not given to us to know when we will die. We may die tomorrow. Or we may die many years from now. We don't know what inflation will do to our savings and retirement plans. More examples of the built-in ambiguity of life could easily be given.

If you tolerate ambiguity only with great difficulty, this will generate considerable anxiety. It may also generate phobic behavior characterized by compulsive avoidance of risk in an effort to control anxiety. It is important to realize that the best way to reduce the existential anxiety associated with the ambiguous nature of life is to accept the ambiguity and learn to tolerate it. It is a fact, not just for you, but for all of us. Look for ways to live with uncertainty. The various suggestions given in this book ought to be of substantial help. And that includes the next suggestion.

DISCOVERING COURAGE

Discover Your Existential Courage. What is existential courage? The theologian Paul Tillich called it *the courage to be.* It is the courage to face life with all its ups and downs, with all its vagaries, with all of its uncertainties.

And how can you discover your existential courage? The answer is that if you look for it you will find it. Most of us discover that we can bear up, that we can carry our burden, if we must. We often suffer the greatest anxiety and worry not when things are going badly, but when things are going well. Apprehension is an emotion associated with what might happen, not with what is actually happening.

Borrow courage from the fact that if and when the chips are down, you will almost certainly have what it takes to keep on going. Tell yourself, "I have the courage to live. I am as suited for life as the next person. I come through for myself and others when I have to." Believe these statements and they become a self-fulfilling prophecy.

Existential courage is not something you learn or acquire. It has been built into your being by God or nature in order to allow you to cope with life. You have it the way you have hands and feet. But you have to *know* you have it. That is why I speak of *discovering* your courage. It's there. Dag Hammarskjöld, a former United Nations secretary-general, said, "Life only demands from you the strength you possess."

≋≋ ≋≋ ≋≋ ≋≋ ≋≋ ≋≋ ≋≋ ≋≋

EMBRACING LIFE

Embrace Life. The German philosopher Arthur Schopenhauer believed that beneath everything, under all that we see and know, is the will to exist. It is this will that creates not only life, but also rocks, oceans, and suns. And Schopenhauer argues that the will to exist is evil. It is evil because it brings death, pain, and suffering. Better, he thought, that there is nothing rather than there is something.

You would think that looking at life this way, Schopenhauer would recommend suicide. But no. He said that suicide of the individual would only strengthen the underlying will to exist that pervades the entire world and universe. It's somewhat like trying to kill devil grass by cutting off the surface growth. The more you cut it, the more the devil grass spreads. You have to dig it out by the roots. By the same logic, you could only destroy the will to exist by getting at its roots. And you can't. It's beyond the scope of human power.

Consequently, Schopenhauer thought that we should just make the best of a bad lot. And in order to do this the only answer was to take some satisfaction in those things and events that posses beauty, such as art and music. As it turns out Schopenhauer actually lived a long, comfortable life. (He inherited a generous sum of money and property.) And he died at the age of seventy-two.

The trouble is that he lived the life of a sourpuss. He was grouchy and pessimistic. He looked down on other people, thinking them intellectually inferior to him. He never married or had a family. His relationships with the opposite sex were emotionally distant. He lived, but he did not embrace life. He simply endured it.

If a person is going to live anyway, doesn't it make more sense to embrace life?

SERIOUSNESS

Don't Take Life Too Seriously. Life is a serious matter. As already noted, it is full of risks and dangers. (However, it should also be noted that it is full of challenges, opportunities, and potential joys.) Being a serious matter, it seems like paradoxical advice to say, "Don't take life too seriously." However, here is the critical point: *Life is too serious a matter to take too seriously.* Because life is real and earnest you want to lighten its load. And one important way to do this is to maintain your sense of humor, to smile, to be entertained by a laughable situation or a good joke.

Over the years I have had a number of blind students in my college classes. I have been struck by the fact that they are almost always cheerful and have a ready sense of humor. They have learned to cope with a very serious matter, losing their eyesight, by carrying life more lightly than many people who have no physical disability at all.

The Last Word

Existential anxiety, anxiety arising from the very roots of life itself, cannot be completely done away with. Nonetheless, the way in which you choose to take life, your attitude and outlook, will determine whether or not you make existential anxiety into an insufferable psychological state or reduce it to a tolerable level. The suggestions made in this chapter, if applied with a will, can help you face life and manage your own existential anxiety.

Key Points to Remember

▢⊸   *Existential anxiety* is the name given to the kind of anxiety that is woven into the very fabric of life.

□— Because the future is by definition to some degree uncertain, we all worry.

□— Accept the fact that we are prone to illness and disease.

□— Accept the fact that we all age.

□— Accept the fact that you too will die.

□— Let go of impossible demands.

□— Assert that you have a free will.

□— Learn to tolerate ambiguity.

□— Discover your existential courage.

□— Embrace life.

□— Don't take life too seriously.

□— The suggestions made in this chapter, if applied with a will, can help you face life and manage your own existential anxiety.

8 PSYCHOTHERAPY: THE TALKING CURE

If you have made a sincere effort to apply the suggestions given in this book, and do not feel that you are bringing anxiety and worry under adequate control, then it is time to consider psychotherapy.

Psychotherapy is sometimes informally called "the talking cure" because it attempts to improve mental and emotional health by a special kind of conversation. This conversation takes place over a series of sessions with a qualified therapist. The term *psychotherapy* implies treatment without drugs.

The aim of this chapter is to help you become a better consumer. You want to be sure to find a therapist who is effective. And you want to have some idea of what will take place in therapy.

Psychotherapists

The first thing you want to do when you start looking for a psychotherapist is to be sure that you are avoiding the quacks. A quack is a person who is filled with confidence, has little or no training, and works semilegally under a business license, not a state professional license. In most states quacks can't call themselves "psychiatrists" or "psychologists." However, they can give themselves imaginative names such as "holistic healer," "mental specialist," and "soul explorer." Just be sure to be on guard. Remember the phrase *caveat emptor*, or "buyer beware."

As indicated above, make sure your psychotherapist is fully qualified and holds a state license to practice. There are three kinds of licensed psychotherapists:

(1) psychiatrists, (2) clinical psychologists, and (3) clinical social workers. *Psychiatrists* are medical doctors. They hold the M.D. (medical doctor) degree and have completed a hospital residency in psychiatry. They are extensively trained to work with severe mental disorders, and they are legally qualified to prescribe drugs. *Clinical psychologists* hold the Ph.D. (doctor of philosophy) degree, and have had extensive course work and supervised training in psychotherapy. *Clinical social workers* hold the M.S.W (master's in social work) degree, and have also had extensive course work and supervised training in psychotherapy. Beyond the above simple facts, the differences among the three kinds of therapists blur. In practice, much depends on the individual's own personality and approach to psychotherapy.

Today's psychotherapists, unlike psychotherapists of the past, take a multimodal approach. A *multimodal approach* picks and chooses among several basic approaches to psychotherapy the specific treatment, or mode, that best fits a given patient. Seldom today does a psychotherapist wear a specific hat such as "psychoanalyst" or "behavior therapist." It is more common for the therapist to *use* psychoanalytic techniques, behavioral ones, or others depending on the nature of a presenting problem.

It is, of course, true that your therapist may favor one approach over another to some degree. Again, this depends to some extent on his or her training as well as assumptions he or she makes about the nature of mental health problems.

Consequently, it will be of value for you to be conversant with the principal approaches used in psychotherapy.

The Psychodynamic Approach

The psychodynamic approach was pioneered by Sigmund Freud in the framework of classical psychoanalysis. The *psychodynamic approach* assumes that the self is a battlefield, and that many mental and emotional problems have roots in one's unconscious mental life. Chapter 3 was informed by the psychodynamic approach.

Freud believed that forbidden wishes banished to the unconscious domain cause most of our neurotic anxiety. Like naughty children sent to a room, they bang around and raise a fuss until they are let out. Similarly, aggressive impulses and sexual impulses that are "not nice" or looked down upon by family and tradition, have a way of wanting to express themselves. If you are a highly traditional or extremely socialized person, these impulses will terrify you. Notice the word that I just used: *Terrify*. And this can of course be a source of anxiety. From a strictly

Freudian point of view, the person who worries to excess is actually terrified of his or her own repressed impulses.

The aim of a psychodynamic approach is not, of course, to let the repressed impulses out so that they can run amok and destroy your life. On the contrary, the aim is to get you to know the impulses, to acquaint yourself with their nature, to examine them in the light of consciousness. In this manner they can be stabilized and brought, so to speak, to heel. The idea is for you to control them, not for them to control you.

The principal technique recommended by Freud for exploring the unconscious is free association. *Free association* is a strategy characterized by talking seemingly at random, without apparent rhyme or reason. The patient reclines on a couch, looking away from the therapist, and often gazes at a blank wall. The verbalizations seem chaotic and disordered, but the assumption is that they have an unconscious connection, a thread of meaning. This thread is followed until an interpretation can be made and one can gain greater access to unconscious motives.

Although free association is the classical way to explore the unconscious, it can in practice be done in many ways. Freud himself pioneered the analysis of slips of the tongue, known as Freudian slips. He also suggested that the analysis of dreams was a royal road to the unconscious domain.

Unconscious content can be obtained in other ways. Often a contemporary psychotherapist will simply engage the client in a series of face-to-face discussions about his or her childhood, attitudes toward parents, and life in general. Many repressed ideas and wishes tend to emerge for discussion and interpretation, particularly if the client is emotionally troubled. And, of course, a majority of clients who seek psychotherapy on their own *are* emotionally troubled, or they wouldn't be bothering to come to the therapist's office.

The virtue of taking a psychodynamic approach in therapy is that it gives the client insight. *Insight* is experienced as a sudden burst of self-understanding in connection with one or several unconscious motives and emotional conflicts. A given insight may not be very large. It could be compared to a small light being turned on. However, insights tend to be retained. The light stays turned on. Psychotherapy often consists of a series of such insights until the mental illumination grows to be quite significant. This illumination helps to set the individual free from self-defeating patterns of thought and behavior. In your case, such illumination can help to free you from chronic worry.

Although insight *is* important, frequently it is not sufficient to bring about behavioral change. It may be, and often is, an important first step. However, modern psychotherapists often focus on the importance of habits, and this focus is associated with the behavioral approach.

The Behavioral Approach

The behavioral approach to psychotherapy asserts that many maladaptive patterns of behavior, including chronic worry, are *learned*. They are acquired through experience. And they are reinforced because they have psychological payoffs valued by the troubled person. Consequently, they are difficult to break or give up.

An example of a valued payoff is the kind of avoidance behavior associated with a phobic reaction. (Examples were given in Chapter 4.) Every time you respond to an irrational fear and avoid its source, you experience a reduction in anxiety. Every time it is experienced, this quick relief strengthens the maladaptive habit. And you get more and more locked into the habit. Obviously, it is next to impossible to break such a pattern with brute willpower.

And, as already indicated, insight isn't enough. You may know *why* you are doing something, but you don't know *how* to do anything about it.

The behavioral approach supplies the *how*.

The kinds of ideas and suggestions made in chapter 4 are incorporated into psychotherapy, giving the client a practical handle on his or her problems. The individual can come to practical grips with nagging worry and persistent anxiety through specific behavior modification strategies.

The hope of the behavioral approach is that what has been learned can be unlearned. It is not a false hope. It is a real hope.

The Cognitive Approach

The cognitive approach is based on the viewpoint that "thinking makes it so." Put in the most straightforward terms, if you think, "I have a headache. I wonder what it means? I've been having too many headaches lately. Maybe I'm getting a brain tumor," then you will feel *anxiety*. If on the other hand, you think, "I have a headache. Everyone gets one once in a while. I probably don't get any more than anyone else," you will feel calm. The very thoughts induce a soothing emotional state.

Therapists who take a cognitive approach assume that you don't have to let thoughts run wild through your head. You can learn to control them. You can apply your intelligence and your will and *reflect* upon your thoughts. (This approach informed Chapter 6.)

A psychotherapist using the cognitive approach will help you to target persistent cognitive distortions, errors you tend to make over and over again in your way of thinking about life and the world. Also, he or she will suggest explicit ways of changing your thought patterns *directly*.

In recent years, the behavioral approach and the cognitive approach have been combined to form a relatively new approach. This approach is called cognitive-behavior modification. *Cognitive-behavior modification* assumes that thoughts, like actions, are learned. Maladaptive thoughts, the kind that produce unnecessary anxiety, can be unlearned like any other behavior. Various strategies are employed. They are similar to those identified in chapter 6.

The Humanistic Approach

The humanistic approach is more correctly called the *humanistic-existential approach* because it incorporates understandings derived from European existential psychology. For convenience, it will be simply referred to as the humanistic approach.

The humanistic approach is characterized by several important assumptions. Two will be identified in this section. First, you have a free will. You can make real choices and take control of your life. You are not a pawn of fate. You really *can* learn to pull your own strings. The assumption of free will cannot be proven philosophically to everyone's satisfaction. However, it can be asserted. If it is asserted, and acted upon, it becomes psychologically real. Using the free will assumption in psychotherapy, your therapist will help you to find ways to become the master of your own fate, including the master of the hobgoblins of excessive anxiety.

Second, you have an inborn need to become the person you were meant to become. The psychologist Abraham Maslow, a principal founder of humanistic psychology, called this *self-actualization*. Self-actualization is an inborn striving process in which you attempt to shape yourself and your life in a manner conforming to your highest aspirations and fondest dreams. The psychological pressure to live up to your potentialities can cause anxiety and worry. Consequently, because of a lack of self-confidence, there is a strong tendency in many of us to avoid really working on making our talents and aptitudes into realities. Your therapist will help you rediscover your fondest dreams and encourage you to bring the seeds of your deepest being into fruition. This will help to quell the flames of existential anxiety surrounding a sense of failure.

The assumptions of humanistic psychology were incorporated into chapter 6.

Biofeedback Training

Biofeedback training is a therapeutic tool that makes it possible to gain almost direct control over anxiety. The training is based on the well-known principle of *knowledge of results*. Whenever we are learning, we want to find out how we are doing. If you bowl, and want to improve your game, you'll be interested in your score. It would be terribly difficult to learn touch typing without a ribbon in your machine or your monitor turned on. Biofeedback training provides knowledge of results. When results change in a desired direction, you find this psychologically rewarding, and learning is hastened.

You will recall from chapter 5 that muscle relaxation is incompatible with anxiety. In biofeedback training, a receiving electrode is held against a selected muscle with the aid of a band. An electronic device provides you with an easy-to-read display of muscle tension. You are instructed to reduce the level of displayed tension. The process is speeded up if you use self-hypnosis or autogenic training. (Again, see Chapter 5.) However, even if you just go at it by trial and error, you will develop thoughts and images, under your voluntary control, that will bring about relaxation. Note that relaxation of a muscle is normally thought to be involuntary; however, through biofeedback training this conventional barrier has been overcome. Biofeedback training is sometimes called *electronic yoga* or *instant Zen*.

Biofeedback training is long past the experimental stage. It is available in many hospitals and clinics as a kind of adjunct therapy. Your psychotherapist should be able to provide you with information pertinent to your area.

The Last Word

Psychotherapy and self-help do not contradict each other. Instead, they tend to go together. When you go to a therapist, you do not take your mind for "fixing" the way you take your car to a mechanic. You can't just be passive and let the therapist do something to you. You have to cooperate, get involved, and in fact be the principal partner in your own therapy. In one sense all psychotherapy is self-directed therapy. The therapist is a facilitator who makes the recovery process take place with greater certainty and effectiveness. Be assured that psychotherapy, with your genuine involvement in it, is very likely to be effective in the treatment of chronic worry. Indeed, the first twentieth-century psychotherapy, psychoanalysis, was designed to treat precisely symptoms arising from persistent anxiety. So you can be confident that psychotherapy is very likely to help you dispel the dark clouds of useless worry and replace them with the sunlit days of a more self-assured way of thinking and living.

Key Points to Remember

□—₥ Psychotherapy is sometimes informally called "the talking cure" because it attempts to improve mental and emotional health by a special kind of conversational approach.

□—₥ Avoid quacks who profess to offer psychotherapy.

□—₥ The three kinds of licensed psychotherapists are: (1) psychiatrists, (2) clinical psychologists, and (3) clinical social workers.

□—₥ Today's psychotherapists tend to take a *multimodal approach*, an approach that picks and chooses among several basic approaches to psychotherapy.

◘⟶ The *psychodynamic approach* assumes that the self is a battlefield, and that many mental and emotional problems have roots in one's unconscious mental life.

◘⟶ *Free association* is a strategy characterized by talking seemingly at random, without apparent rhyme or reason. The strategy is used to probe the unconscious domain.

◘⟶ *Insight* is experienced as a sudden burst of self-understanding in connection with one or several unconscious motives and emotional conflicts.

◘⟶ The *behavioral approach* to psychotherapy asserts that many maladaptive patterns of behavior, including chronic worry, are learned.

◘⟶ The *cognitive approach* to psychotherapy is based on the viewpoint that "thinking makes it so." In other words, thoughts induce emotional states.

◘⟶ *Cognitive-behavior modification* combines the behavioral and cognitive approaches.

◘⟶ The *humanistic approach* assumes that you have a free will. It also assumes that you have an inborn need to become the person you were meant to be. This need is identified with the term *self-actualization*.

◘⟶ *Biofeedback training* is a therapeutic tool that makes it possible to gain almost direct control over anxiety.

◘⟶ Psychotherapy, with your genuine involvement, is very likely to be effective in the treatment of chronic worry.

9 TRANQUILIZERS: THE PROS AND CONS OF ANTIANXIETY DRUGS

Drug therapy has a proper place in the fight against anxiety and chronic worry. As a treatment avenue, it is appropriate when neither attempts at self-help nor psychotherapy seem to bring adequate improvement in one's mental and emotional state.

The aim of this chapter is to provide some basic information on the use of tranquilizers to treat intractable anxiety.

The kinds of drugs described can be prescribed only by a licensed physician. Psychiatrists are licensed physicians. Clinical psychologists and clinical social workers are not.

Kinds of Tranquilizers

In the past, a class of drugs known as *barbiturates* was used to treat anxiety. These are usually avoided today for several reasons. Principal among these is that they are habit forming and consequently have a high addictive potential.

A distinction is made in drug therapy between the major tranquilizers and the minor tranquilizers. The *major tranquilizers* are used to treat psychotic disorders such as schizophrenia. Persons suffering from schizophrenia tend to have delusions and sometimes hallucinations. This is, of course, a severe mental illness, often requiring hospitalization.

On the other hand, the *minor tranquilizers* are used to treat excessive anxiety. This may result from a neurotic process. Or, possibly, in some cases there can be a biological basis. (This was explored in chapter 2.) Whatever the reason, psychological or biological, the drug may be prescribed if the anxiety seems to be intractable and otherwise resistant to treatment.

Minor tranquilizers belong to the drug class benzodiazepines. *Benzodiazepines* are sedative-hypnotic agents capable of lowering central nervous system arousal. One of their effects is that they induce muscle relaxation. In addition to their specific usage in the treatment of anxiety, they may be prescribed to treat muscle spasms, convulsive disorders, and sleep disorders.

In view of the fact that anxiety is a very common symptom, the benzodiazepines tend to be prescribed quite often. It is estimated that more than fifty million prescriptions are written each year in the United States.

The term *benzodiazepines*, appearing without capitalization, refers to the generic, or chemical, name of this class of drugs. However, when you see a drug name capitalized, it refers to the copyrighted trade name of the drug. Consequently, it is trade names that are advertised, and that you are more likely to have heard about. Also, the prescription is often written in terms of its trade name. Benzodiazepines are marketed under approximately fifty different trade names.

Here are some of the trade names: (1) Ativan, (2) Centrax, (3) Dalmane, (4) Klonopin, (5) Librium, (6) Rivotril, (7) Serax, (8) Tranxene, (9) Valium, and (10) Xanax.

Benzodiazepines are either long acting or short acting. *Long-acting benzodiazepines* tend to have persistent pharmacological effects for several days after the last dose is taken. *Short-acting benzodiazepines* tend to be cleared from the body quickly.

An advantage of a short-acting tranquilizer is that if one wants to be completely rid of its sedative-hypnotic effect during the day, it may be taken in the late evening or at bedtime. When the individual wakes up there will probably be little or no drug in the system. On the other hand, much of the tranquilizing effect will also be lost from a strictly chemical point of view. Nonetheless, there may be a beneficial psychological carry over.

In the case of long-acting benzodiazepines, it is usually asserted that withdrawal from the drug is somewhat easier because the drug, from a chemical point of view, is self-tapering.

Long-acting benzodiazepines include Valium, Librium, Tranxene, Klonopin, and Centrax. Short-acting benzodiazepines include Ativan, Serax, and Xanax. Whether or not to prescribe a long-acting or a short-acting benzodiazepine is a matter to be discussed between the physician and the patient. Individual differences play a large part in the making the appropriate decision.

PROS OF TRANQUILIZERS

Here are some of the pros of taking tranquilizers:

1. As already indicated, tranquilizers may come to your rescue when nothing else seems to be working. They do have a distinct place in the treatment of intractable anxiety and chronic worry.

2. Taken without other drugs, benzodiazepines tend to be physiologically safe. (For exceptions, see "cons" below.) They have a low level of toxicity. For example, taken alone, an overdose will not be life threatening. It is doubtful that they will prematurely age you or induce a disease process.

3. Tranquilizers have close to a thirty-year track record as a prescription drug. Consequently, the medical profession has a large base of information to work from. They are not experimental drugs with unknown long-term effects.

4. Tranquilizers almost always achieve their goal. Most persons who take them report a reduction in anxiety. Relief tends to be rapid.

5. It is possible, after a period of trial and error, to establish a fixed dosage level. Fortunately, a drug tolerance, which would require ever-larger doses, does not build up. The same amount of the drug continues to provide relief for many months, or even years.

6. The vast majority of people who take tranquilizers for relief from anxiety do not abuse them.

7. Withdrawal from benzodiazepines does not precipitate a medical emergency. Cramps, sweats, headaches, and delusions are not likely to accompany cessation of the drug.

CONS OF TAKING TRANQUILIZERS

Here are some of the cons of taking tranquilizers:

1. Tranquilizers are sedative-hypnotic agents. Consequently, they may to some extent impair one's alertness and general level of arousal during the day. This is particularly true if one is taking a benzodiazepine with a long-acting effect. Ability to pay attention or solve a problem may be somewhat handicapped.

2. Although, as indicated above, benzodiazepines tend to be physiologically safe, usage for long periods of time may interfere with liver function. This needs to be evaluated with a physician.

3. The prescription of benzodiazepines needs to be very carefully evaluated, and perhaps avoided

completely, if the individual has kidney disease, lung disease, diabetes, or glaucoma.

4. If you have myasthenia gravis, you should not take a benzodiazepine. Myasthenia gravis is a disorder of the muscles, particularly of the head area. It is most likely an autoimmune disorder in which the body attacks itself.

5. Benzodiazepines may have an adverse effect on fetal development. Pregnant women should avoid taking them.

6. Tranquilizers interact with alcohol in such a way as to amplify the sedative effect of both drugs. For example, a person who has had two highballs and who is also taking a tranquilizer may make a very dangerous driver.

7. Unpleasant side effects may occur in some individuals. The following are relatively infrequent, but they do occur: (1) confusion, (2) rash, (3) itch, (4) dry mouth, (5) upset stomach, (6) unpleasant dreams, and (7) headaches.

8. In a relatively small number of cases, the taking of a benzodiazepine may interfere with sexual desire.

9. Older people do not tend to tolerate benzodiazepines as well as younger people.

10. Taking a tranquilizer may "take the wind out of your sails" in connection with both helping yourself and motivation in psychotherapy. A tranquilizer can be so effective that you get mentally lazy and do not feel the impetus to develop your own resources. There may be a "so what?" attitude toward the various coping strategies indicated in this book. The same tends to be true of psychotherapy. The client who no longer suffers from anxiety may not feel that psychotherapy is

important any longer. Consequently, underlying problems may remain unsolved and untreated.

11. As already indicated, withdrawal from a tranquilizer does not precipitate a medical emergency. But this does not mean that withdrawal is easy. On the contrary, although it appears that little or no physiological dependency is associated with tranquilizers, a psychological dependency is. Consequently, persons often find it very difficult and unpleasant to give up tranquilizers.

For one or several of the above reasons, taking a tranquilizer may not be the right thing for you to do. That is why benzodiazepines are prescription drugs. The decision to take them has to be carefully evaluated with a responsible medical doctor who also has psychiatric training. The professional person most qualified to do this is a psychiatrist.

Lines of Defense

Think of your personal war on anxiety and chronic worry like war in general. There are several lines of defense. Your first line of defense is yourself. You want to do all that you can to develop your own resources, to cultivate your inner strengths. This is the principal way in which you can say to yourself, "I am in charge. I own my own life."

The second line of defense is psychotherapy. In psychotherapy you do not give up your autonomy. You are still in charge. You and the therapist are cooperative partners working to improve your mental and emotional health. When psychotherapy terminates, you come out of it with insights and learning that can help you to cope for many years to come.

The third line of defense is drug therapy. If neither self-help strategies nor psychotherapy are reasonably effective, then the taking of a tranquilizer may very well be indicated. But note that drug therapy is a *third* line of defense. Unfortunately, some people think of it as a *first* line of defense. And before they have even considered the first two lines, they are seeking drug therapy.

This book has been written with the aim of helping you consolidate your own strengths. Its underlying theme is intelligent self-reliance.

The Last Word

The decision to embark on a course of drug therapy for anxiety and worry should not be made lightly. If anxiety seems to be intractable and worry chronic, then sometimes drug therapy can be very beneficial. This chapter has given you some basic information that will help you evaluate the pros and cons of drug therapy. Don't hesitate to discuss the advantages and disadvantages of drug therapy with a qualified medical doctor.

Key Points to Remember

□— Drug therapy has a proper place in the fight against anxiety and chronic worry.

□— Barbiturates used to be prescribed to treat anxiety. Today they are seldom prescribed for this purpose.

□— The *major tranquilizers* are used to treat psychotic disorders such as schizophrenia.

□— The *minor tranquilizers* are used to treat excessive anxiety.

□— Minor tranquilizers belong to the drug class benzodiazepines. *Benzodiazepines* are sedative-hypnotic agents capable of lowering central nervous system arousal.

□━ The term *benzodiazepines*, appearing without capitalization, refers to the generic, or chemical, name of this class of drugs.

□━ Some of the capitalized trade names associated with the benzodiazepines include Centrax, Valium, and Xanax.

□━ Benzodiazepines are either long acting or short acting.

□━ Seven pros of taking tranquilizers were listed. The principal one of these is that tranquilizers may come to your rescue when nothing else seems to be working.

□━ Eleven cons of taking tranquilizers were listed. One of these is that because these drugs are sedative-hypnotic agents they may impair to some extent one's alertness and general level of arousal during the day.

□━ The three lines of defense in your personal war on anxiety and chronic worry are: (1) your own resources, (2) psychotherapy, and (3) drug therapy.

□━ The decision to embark on a course of drug therapy for anxiety and worry should not be made lightly.

10 LIFE CAN BE BETTER: A SEVEN-STEP ANTIWORRY PROGRAM

You have read the book, and you are convinced that there is much you can do for yourself to manage your tendency toward excessive worry and, consequently, make your life better.

But where do you start?

As you know, the book makes many suggestions. There are a variety of ways to slay, or at least wound, the monster of unnecessary anxiety. Think of these suggestions as your armory of weapons.

But which weapon should you use first?

There are two basic approaches you can take. Either approach may be helpful, and the approach you select should be based on your own perception of your particular personality and your individual needs. Also, the approaches are not mutually exclusive, and can be combined.

The Need-Demand Approach

The first approach is the *need-demand approach*. In the need-demand approach you allow your own most pressing worry tendencies to determine which self-directed coping strategy you will apply first, or at any given time. Flip through the book and highlight or otherwise mark an anxiety-arousing behavior that seems to be similar to something you do. (It is quite possible that you have already done so.) There is bound to be more than one time when the book's examples seem to be mirror images of your own behavior. Pick one that seems particularly outstanding to you, and then apply the associated strategy.

For example, let's say that you seem to find it almost impossible to relax, and you know that this is aggravating your worry habit. You decide to select the autogenic training method of inducing relaxation. Practice the method for about a week or ten days. Assuming you get good results, you will be ready to move on and use another strategy. Again, use the need-demand approach in order to make a selection of this second strategy.

In this manner you can proceed through the book in a superficially random fashion. But the track is not really random. It is determined by your own most pressing needs. You let them demand the strategy of the moment.

I suggest that you keep the book handy for future reference. When you feel the need to control a worry tendency, turn to the book and find a strategy that will help you.

The Systematic Approach

The systematic approach is the basis of the *seven-step antiworry program*. Using the program, you approach chronic worrying in an orderly, organized manner. The program is based on the "divide and conquer" principle. You chop up the worry monster into manageable little monsters, and then you, slay, or at least subdue, each smaller creature one by one.

The chapters in the book have been arranged in a logical sequence. Consequently, if you approach working on worry in terms of the book's predetermined sequence, you will be on solid ground.

The application of the program is not time consuming. So don't rationalize and say to yourself, "I like the ideas in the book. I'll get to them when I'm not so busy." In most cases the strategies require no major alterations in your lifestyle nor excessive time-out periods from a daily routine. On the contrary, they are designed to fit in readily to the kind of busy, demanding lives that so many of us lead these days.

STEP I

Turn to chapter 2, "Exploring Bodily Processes." I am assuming, of course, that you have already read the book. Now scan through the suggestions made under the heading "What You Can Do for Yourself." Look for one that sort of pops out, that seems to say, "Try me." Follow your inclination. Be a little intuitive about this because an intuition usually represents an amalgam of both rational thought processes and subconscious data processing.

Let's say that a suggestion relating to the control of hypoglycemia, or low blood sugar, makes an impression on you. You think that it is a possibility that your eating habits combined with a tendency toward hypoglycemia are aggravating your tendency to worry. Apply the suggestion for about one week. The important point is to *focus on this suggestion and only this suggestion*. Give no conscious attention to the other strategies in the book.

The idea is to have a success, to boost your sense of self-esteem and the conviction that you can actually do something for yourself.

After one week has elapsed, assess your improvement. If there has been any improvement at all in your behavior, define this as a success. You don't have to lick the problem once and for all. Don't think in terms of cure; think in terms of improvement. Avoid either-or thinking about results, or, being a chronic worrier, you will almost always see failure instead of success.

Stop working consciously on Step 1. Allow your subconscious to take over, and turn consciously to Step 2.

STEP 2

Turn to chapter 3, "Our Emotional Conflicts." Chapter 3 contains self-directed coping strategies that will help you reduce anxiety arising from deeper levels of your personality.

Turn to the heading "Ending the Civil War With Yourself." Select a suggestion in accordance with the procedure described in Step 1. Follow the same general recommendations as those made in Step 1. Again, keep in mind that you are looking for improvement, not a complete and final solution. Again, one week of focused effort is enough. Now turn to Step 3.

STEP 3

Turn to chapter 4, "The Worry Habit." Chapter 4 offers you practical ways to modify the kinds of learned reactions that support your worry behavior.

Turn to the heading "Unmaking the Worry Habit." Select a suggestion in accordance with the procedure described in Step 1. Apply one week of focused effort to the suggestion. Again, don't expect miracles, but do expect good results in a positive direction. Don't look for one big success, but for small successes. I will stop repeating this point here, and you can assume that it is implicit in the subsequent steps. Now turn to Step 4.

STEP 4

Turn to chapter 5, "Inducing Relaxation." As you will recall, relaxation of the muscles is antagonistic to anxiety.

Relaxing is a counterconditioning strategy that genuinely helps you to extinguish excessive anxiety and compulsive worry.

Find the heading "Methods." Select a method in accordance with the procedure described in Step 1. Follow the other recommendations outlined in Step 1. After one week of focused work, turn to Step 5.

STEP 5

Turn to chapter 6, "Our Mental Lives." This chapter is based on the idea that common cognitive distortions (warped thoughts), tend to readily create irrational fears, excessive anxiety, and useless worries. Anxiety can be reduced by challenging these reactive thought processes.

Find the heading "Self-Directed Mental Strategies." Select a strategy in accordance with the procedure described in Step 1. Follow the other recommendations outlined in Step 1. After one week of focused attention, turn to Step 6.

STEP 6

Turn to chapter 7, "Everybody Worries." Chapter 7 is based on the idea that existential anxiety, anxiety arising from the very nature and fabric of life itself, is to some degree inevitable. However, even existential anxiety is subject to psychological management.

Turn to the heading "Reducing Existential Anxiety." Select a strategy in accordance with the procedure described in Step 1. Follow the other recommendations outlined in Step 1. After one week of focused attention, turn to Step 7.

STEP 7

Give yourself a one-week break. Make no conscious effort to apply any of the suggestions in the book. If you have gathered some momentum, and are using some of the strategies as a new semiautomatic tendency, by all means continue. You want to make a better way of behaving into a set of new habits. But willed behavior is not habit. Willed behavior requires effort. Give your willed behavior, your intentional application of strategies, a rest.

Now seven weeks have elapsed since you started the program. Assess where you are. If you feel that you have experienced enough improvement to be able to say, "Excessive worry is no longer a problem in my life," then give yourself a pat on the back and enjoy your sense of well being.

On the other hand, if you feel that you want to continue working on worry management, then turn to Step 1 and repeat the entire program. This time you may, of course, be using different strategies from those you selected the first time around. This is appropriate and recommended.

Repeat the program as often as you feel it is necessary to do so. Perhaps you will go for six months or a year without the feeling that you need the program. But if and when worry seems to be getting out of hand in your life, remember that the program is always there, available to you, in the form of this book.

The Last Word

I hope that you will make *Stop Worrying* a permanent part of your library. Think of it as helpful friend that you can call upon any time you want to.

Key Points to Remember

☐━ There are two basic approaches you can take in your general efforts to cope with excessive anxiety and chronic worry. These are the need-demand approach and the systematic approach.

☐━ In the *need-demand approach*, you allow your own most pressing worry tendencies to determine which self-directed coping strategy you will apply first, or at any given time.

☐━ In the *systematic approach*, you follow the *seven-step antiworry program* outlined in the chapter.